OUT OF THE

DARKNESS

AND INTO

HIS LIGHT

JACK BERNARD BURNS

WESTBOW
PRESS®
A DIVISION OF THOMAS NELSON
& ZONDERVAN

WestBow Press books may be ordered through booksellers or by contacting:

WestBow Press
A Division of Thomas Nelson & Zondervan
1663 Liberty Drive
Bloomington, IN 47403
www.westbowpress.com
844-714-3454

ISBN: 978-1-6642-2399-8 (sc)
ISBN: 978-1-6642-2400-1 (e)

Library of Congress Control Number: 2021903367

Print information available on the last page.

WestBow Press rev. date: 03/01/2021

Dedicated first to my Lord and Savior, Jesus Christ, and His Glory; second to my wife, Janet Irene Burns; and third to my son, Alex Ryan Burns, and my daughters, Angela Louise Burns, Tracy Lynn Chapman, and Angela Marie Brown (deceased), and all my grandsons and great-grandchildren.

Whoever prints this book may not agree with this, my personal witness and testimony of my life; however, I give to them the right to disagree and not be held accountable for the contents that I write about in my autobiography.

FOREWORD

Some of my earliest memories revolve around visits to our Church by Missionaries who had answered God's call to be His witnesses in foreign lands. I vividly recall the clicking and flashing of the colorful slide presentations, (for those folks younger than I am "slide presentation" may require a little bit of explanation), and the various native clothing items and artifacts displayed at the front of the sanctuary. These powerful presentations made the lives these committed men and women lived in various locations around the world come alive to a small-town young boy. I'm glad I was raised in a mission-minded Church, which strongly supported mission work around the world. And I'm thankful I learned to genuinely appreciate the personal sacrifice these missionaries exhibited by their faithfulness to serve God wherever He called them.

My admirations and appreciations for men and women who were called by God to serve as missionaries continued to grow throughout my life. I always counted it an honor and a privilege to meet and spend time with them. Little did I know that one day, God had plans to bring an SBC Foreign Mission couple to be part of our local Church.

As I had the privilege to meet and get to know Jack and Janet Burns, I saw in them the faithful commitment and the resolve that appeared to be consistent in all the missionaries I'd ever met. I loved to hear them share stories of what God had done for them and through them in their time spent in Brazil. Then, God called them into service again to South Korea, and later to South Africa. With each deployment came even more fascinating and remarkable accounts and testimonies.

And, whenever Jack was home, and had available time, he was always eager to join in any mission projects we were doing through our local Church. When he and Janet finally retired from their SBC mission work, Jack was always the first person to sign up for whatever outreach project we were planning. These have included dozens of Prison Ministry events, ministering to incarcerated men and women all across North Carolina, multiple mission trips to KY, Eastern NC, two mission trips to the Czech Republic, and nearly a dozen trips to Russia. I can't adequately describe how significant it has been to have a "Genuine Foreign Missionary" as part of our team on all these excursions.

If there is one trait that stands out in Jack's life, I would undoubtedly say that it is his faithfulness in sharing the gospel of Jesus Christ. No one has ever spent more than a couple of minutes around Jack without hearing how God changed him from a false witness into a born-again Soul Winner. Wherever Jack goes, folks are always amazed at how God has used him and used Janet in such a mighty way. People all over the world are fascinated as Jack recalls some of what he and Janet have been able to witness. Almost invariably, as Jack shares his testimony and accounts of God's greatness, someone will tell him, "You really need to write a book about what God has done in your life."

Well… I think he finally got the message! I believe in addition to the many request from other folks, God finally stepped in and let Jack know it was time to transcribe some of what He had allowed Jack and Janet to witness.

I know you will find this book as fascinating and inspiring as the other folks I've seen touched by Jack's testimony around the world. May reading this book inspire all of us to commit our lives fully to His will and His way, and to embolden us to share the Gospel with everyone we have a chance to meet.

INTRODUCTION

"For God so loved the world that He gave His only begotten Son, that whoever believes in Him should not perish but have everlasting life" (John 3:16 NKJV).[1]

"But you shall receive power when the Holy Spirit has come upon you; and you shall be witnesses to Me in Jerusalem, and in all Judea and Samaria, and to the end of the earth" (Acts 1:8 NKJV).

"Go therefore and make disciples of all the nations, baptizing them in the name of the Father and of the Son and of the Holy Spirit, teaching them to observe all things that I have commanded you; and lo, I am with you always, even to the end of the age" (Matthew 28:18–20 NKJV).

"And I, if I am lifted up from the earth, will draw all peoples to Myself" (John 12: 32 NKJV).

These precious words from my Lord to my heart, which became real and personal to me when I committed my life to believe and to follow Jesus Christ as Lord and Savior of my life on December 21, 1984, have been my decision in life as one of His disciples. I am only one of His children, and I desire to be the best servant of His that I can become. With this in my mind and on my heart and as I seek to do God's will for my life daily, I pray that I will glorify Jesus with this story and in all that I do and say, trusting Him in obedience to His will for my life. I have now come to the time in my life, after saying no to writing my story to my Lord many times over the years, when I have said yes!

---

[1] All Bible scriptures are from the Believer's Study Bible, New King James Version (Thomas Nelson, Inc., 1982).

CHAPTER 1

Growing up in Morehead City for twelve years before moving to Wilmington, North Carolina, where I lived for thirty years, I was raised as a believing and practicing Jehovah's Witness, thanks to my mother. By age six, I was doing missions for the Watchtower Society, going door to door in many areas of eastern North Carolina, and by age ten, I was preparing to learn how to preach through the theocratic ministry school. After I reached the age of fifteen, I became an assistant overseer in a new congregation of Jehovah's Witnesses in Wilmington. And I was used in their conventions in many areas of service.

In 1974, I was judged by three elders in the congregation to be living in sin because of my use of tobacco. Because of my sin, according to these three who saw nothing wrong in their use of alcohol or dishonest business practices, I was disfellowshipped, or excommunicated, by the Watchtower Society. With this decision, I could no longer preach, teach, give prayer, or be spoken to in the fellowship or in public. I was to be shunned until I repented of my use of tobacco before the elders of the congregation. Even my own mother, father, and brother couldn't be seen with me, or they would be excommunicated. Though I was no longer a practicing Jehovah's Witness, I continued to believe their false doctrines. I was still aware of the sin in my life that I could hide from my family and the folks in the Witnesses. But I knew that I was a sinner and needed my sins forgiven by God, so I was lost—although I did not know what that meant at that time. I needed for Father God to forgive me of my sins and to give me His forgiveness, peace in my heart, and a new life. I did not know what to do at the time, but I began to seek the Lord with all of my heart. My life was in turmoil because of my marital problems, which was God's way of totally breaking my will and my spirit in order for the spirit of God to draw me to the Father. I was truly broken in spirit and did not care if I lived or died at that point in time, which was about ten years after I lost everything.

From 1974 until December 21, 1984, I built my life around bowling and other interests to help me find peace. I was using things to help fill the void in my life. Many of my friends were in the bowling alleys of Wilmington and across the South, and I became a leader in the men's associations of Wilmington and the state of North Carolina. It was during this time period that my children, Ryan and Angela Burns, became active in an evangelical Southern Baptist church near our home. Ryan had asked me if he could play softball with some of his friends, and I said yes. I did not know that for him to be able to play on this church team he had to go to this Southern Baptist church, which was across the street from the kingdom hall that I was a leader in. Ryan got saved and began to invite me to church to hear him and Angela sing. Since they were never baptized as Jehovah's Witnesses, they were free to go with their friends and their school bands to play in churches during special times of the year, such as Christmas. They became active in the youth groups, especially the youth choir at Winter Park Baptist Church.

I finally said yes to Ryan's invitation, and I went to Winter Park Baptist Church on a Sunday night. I was scared to death about going to that church because Jehovah's Witnesses are taught that going inside the devil's organization—no matter what kind of evangelical church—would bring the wrath of Jehovah God on you.

As I sat in my car with the fear of man on me, many folks drove up and went into the sanctuary to worship. I thought if I went in with them, God would not kill them to get to me. So I went in, and it wasn't anything that I heard or saw but the truth that I was still alive after I walked out. I thought that since I was still alive, I could go again. It was after this time that I really began to seek the Lord with all of my heart. Since I worked shift work in a large paper mill in Riegelwood, North Carolina, at this time, I could not go to church every time the doors of worship were open. However, a friend of mine invited me to Long Leaf Baptist Church to see and to hear a Christmas cantata and drama on either December 21 or December 22, 1984. My schedule at work allowed me to go on December 21, which would be my first visit to Long Leaf with Pastor Dr. Johnny Hunt leading the service. I can still remember where I was sitting (five rows back on the left side of the sanctuary) and the nine-foot wooden cross above the baptistery.

As I was listening to the gospel message of a loving Savior and Lord whose name is Jesus Christ, I could actually see Jesus on the cross. I heard Him say to my heart, "How much do I love you, Jack? I gave all of myself for you." This broke my heart because I knew that if for nobody else on this earth, Jesus died to pay for my sins. The folk sitting near me said that they could hear me weeping from a broken heart.

When Pastor Johnny gave the invitation to come to Christ, on the platform stood a brother in Christ who played the role of Jesus Christ in the drama. Because I thought that I was to obey Pastor Johnny, I got out of my seat to go to Jesus Christ, trusting Him as my Lord and Savior. It was on

2

my knees behind the sanctuary that Janet Hunt, the pastor's wife, led me in the sinner's prayer. I admitted to Jesus that I was a sinner and could not save myself, and I asked Him to forgive me of my sins and to save me. I asked Jesus to come and live in my heart and life, and I said I would turn from my sin to follow Him as best as I knew how. I then asked Jesus to make a soul winner out of me and to use me wherever He would lead me for His glory and kingdom. I thanked Him for saving me, and when I got up, I was a new creation. The old Jack Burns was dead, and I stood up as a new creature sold out to Jesus to tell the world what He had done for me.

I then began to go to the paper mill and tell those I worked with what Jesus had done for me and that He would do the same for anyone who called on Him in faith. I watched many who were lost and who did not know Him chase believers down and ask how they could have their sins forgiven and know with assurance that they would be in heaven with Jesus. I continued to bowl, and many would ask me what the problem was in my life and how I found peace and joy. I would introduce them to Jesus Christ as their Lord and Savior, who would change their hearts and life, forgive them of their sins, and let them live for all eternity in heaven. I witnessed to fifty-two of these folks and helped them pray to receive Jesus Christ as their Lord and Savior in the first year of my salvation. Two weeks after my public profession of faith in Jesus Christ, I was baptized with believer's baptism.

I personally experienced my sins being washed away as I was buried in Christ and came up out of the water to go and be a light to the world for my Lord and Savior, Jesus Christ. I also began to realize in my heart that I was one of God's church and I needed to talk to Him all the time, as He lived in my heart. I began to read His Word every day so He could speak to me and I could personally be in fellowship with Him. I heard His Word for the first time the right way because His spirit would bring His Word alive to me. I also began to watch evangelical preachers, such as Dr. Charles Stanley, Reverend Billy Graham, and others I had never been allowed to hear as a Witness. I remember praying the sinner's prayer many times until the Holy Spirit told me I had already done this and that once was enough.

Every day with Jesus was life-changing for me, but the evil one began to give me trouble. I was told that the evil one was not happy with my decision to follow Jesus and that I should expect trials and persecution to come. This just proved to me that I belonged to Jesus.

I never had this problem before because the devil and my flesh controlled my life until December 21, 1984. However, Jesus Christ is now my Lord, and only He controls my heart, my will, and my life. At this time, God put two precious godly men in my life to mentor and to grow me in my faith. God used Jim Coates, a precious man of God who was a deacon in Long Leaf Baptist Church, and Pastor Johnny Hunt to grow my faith in many ways. Long Leaf Baptist Church was a CWT witness-training Southern Baptist church, with an active CWT evangelism program to witness about saving faith in Jesus Christ. I knew in my heart that Jehovah God had trained me how to witness the wrong way about knowing Him, so since I was born again as one of His witnesses, and all I had to do for Him was give Jesus away to those who did not know Him personally. I said, "Where do I go, and what do I do, Pastor Johnny?"

I learned how to tell people my story and ask them to ask Jesus to forgive their sins, to let them spend eternity in heaven, and to save them, and He would! Brother Jim Coates loved to visit folks in their homes, in the hospital, and in the rest homes to show the love and grace of a Holy God. He would call me to pray with me and to ask me to go visiting with him, which gave me the opportunity to share my story and to pray for the people. He and his precious wife, Ellen, would include me in their family outings and would love on me with the love of God. Because my family had either left me or would not fellowship with me because of the change in my life, my church family, along with Pastor Johnny Hunt and his family and Jim and Ellen Coates, became my family.

Every year, God would use many folks of His family to help me to grow in my faith and walk within the body of believers, where He would lead me to serve Him. The pastors, the Sunday school teachers, the choir leaders, and the prayer warriors would pour into me what our Lord had poured into them by faith. Beginning in January of 1985, God would bless me and use me to tell how He had saved me in various ways many times during that year. First, Pastor Johnny Hunt had asked me to share my testimony during Baptist men's day in January. He also asked my son, Ryan, to sing before I testified to the folks of Long Leaf Baptist Church. This Sunday morning worship service would be broadcast over the local television program weekly and over the southern part of North Carolina and South Carolina. Never did I know that our Lord would use this personal experience to help lead others to Him by faith. However, when I went to work on the midnight shift at the paper mill in Riegelwood, North Carolina, after the Baptist men's program was televised, two men I worked with told me that they had woken up that Sunday morning after drinking during the night. They listened to the program and heard what Jesus Christ had done for me, and they cleaned up and went to the local Baptist church that Sunday morning and asked Jesus to do for them what He had done for me.

There was joy in heaven that morning because two lost sinners became born-again followers of Jesus Christ as their Lord and Savior. I was so excited because Jesus was now being talked about daily by many of my coworkers who had begun to seek the Lord with all of their hearts for a changed heart and life.

The next great experience came when I went with one of the ministers of Long Leaf who was making a personal visit to a mother and daughter who had been studying with folks of the Jehovah's Witnesses. During one of the CWT home visits, both mother and daughter prayed to receive Jesus Christ as their personal Lord and Savior, and the minister was asked to come and talk to the Witnesses. The minister asked me to go with him on the visit, and instead of us going to defend the decision of the mother and daughter to follow Jesus as born-again believers, Jesus led us to lead the son to saving faith in Jesus Christ. Now the whole family are believers and followers of Jesus Christ. Jesus is now Lord of that household.

There was a divine appointment there, but instead of defending the decision of both mother and daughter, we were to introduce the son to Jesus Christ as His Lord and Savior.

Soon, I was invited to share my testimony in many of the local evangelical Southern Baptist churches and to teach the folks what Jehovah's Witnesses believe and practice. For teaching in this area in churches and in colleges, I was appointed as an interfaith associate of the North America Mission Board in 1985 in the area of Jehovah's Witnesses, and I also have been used in this area in many countries for the International Mission Board of the Southern Baptist Convention since we were appointed as international missionaries in 1996. I also continued to lead people to saving faith in Jesus Christ through the continuous witness training program in Long Leaf Baptist Church and at the local bowling alleys during this time.

Pastor Johnny Hunt asked me to be a messenger for Long Leaf Baptist Church at the Southern Baptist Convention in Dallas, Texas, in June of 1985 to help elect the leaders of our convention to lead us into the future in carrying out our Lord's commands, found in Matthew 28:18–20, and to become Acts 1:8 (NKJV) followers for Jesus Christ. This would bring glory and honor to our Lord and His kingdom. This was an awesome experience for our group and me, as we heard great men of God preach during the Southern Baptist Pastors Conference, including Dr. D. James Kennedy, pastor of First Presbyterian Church of Fort Lauderdale, Florida. We also had the joy of worshiping with First Baptist Church of Dallas, Texas; hearing Zig Ziglar (deceased) teach Sunday School from the sanctuary; and seeing and hearing Dr. W. A. Criswell (deceased), pastor of First Baptist Church, preach on "The Infallible Word of God."

I thought that I was seeing and listening to a prophet of God with his white suit, white shoes, and white hair. After the service, I had the joy of meeting and talking to Zig Ziglar one on one, which blessed my life. In addition to this first time attending a Southern Baptist convention, I also met a close friend from Wilmington, North Carolina, whom I had bowled with, fished with, and partied with in the convention center. He looked at me and said, "Jack, is that you?" and I said, "Royce, is that you?"

We both shared how Jesus had forgiven our sins and had saved us in services in Wilmington, North Carolina, in different churches. Royce (who is now deceased) stated that God had called him to pastor and into His service. He also said that He had attended Fruitland Baptist Bible Institute in Fruitland, North Carolina, in answer to God's call on his life. After completing his preparation for ministry, he had been called by First Baptist Church in Dayton, Ohio, as an associate pastor. This statement took my breath away, and we both said that if God could save us sinners, He could save anyone.

This time in Dallas was an experience used by my Lord to minister to others in a very special way in answer to prayers. I forgot to share a personal experience with my father, Harry Burns, four days before he went to be with Jesus a couple of months prior to this time. I had been trying to share my personal testimony with my father, who was very ill, and my mother and brother, who were still strong followers of the Watchtower Society, would stop me. Finally with him alone in the hospital and free to talk, I shared with him how Jesus had forgiven me of my sins and had saved me. I asked him as I walked through the sinner's prayer, had there ever been a time that he asked Jesus to forgive him of his sins and to save him and become his Lord and Savior? He said yes! I said that he had never told me that before, and he said that I had never asked him that before. What a comfort and joy it was to my heart to know that we would be in heaven together since we both were born-again believers of Jesus Christ! My father died four days later, and the Witnesses did the funeral without letting me say anything since I was disfellowshipped. However, our Lord had me tell all of our family what I had found out about my father's testimony of trusting Jesus by faith, which meant he was in heaven with Jesus. I also told them, "Unless you are born again and become a follower of Jesus Christ, this will be the last time that you will see his body."

My Christian family embraced me with the love of Jesus Christ and took care of me both spiritually and physically. I know that the only thing that separates me from my father is time and space. I will see him again based on God's Word, which brings comfort to my spirit.

As I continued to share my story with local churches, I was invited to Hampstead Baptist Church in Hampstead, North Carolina, to share with the youth and church folk about how Jesus will change your life by forgiving you of your sins and saving you to spend an eternity in heaven with Him. When the invitation was given, many were under conviction but would not respond to Jesus at the time. I felt that I had let my Lord down and was so discouraged for days after this time. However, just a few weeks later, during an evangelistic crusade in July of 1985 that was held in Wilmington, North Carolina, by evangelist Freddie Gage (deceased) of Texas first at the local football stadium and the last two nights in Trask Coliseum on the campus of the University of North Carolina at Wilmington, fifteen of the youth of Hampstead Baptist Church committed their lives to saving faith in Jesus Christ. As I was a counselor during this crusade time, the group came to me after they had gone forward during the invitation time to pray and receive Jesus Christ as their Lord and Savior to tell me that God had used me for the Spirit of God to put them under deep conviction about their sin and life, and they settled the need that night by giving their heart and life to Jesus as their Lord and Savior.

The weeks of the crusade were awesome. As a counselor, I helped people confirm their decision to follow Christ with the rest of their life after they had prayed the sinner's prayer of faith.

One special experience happened on the last night of the crusade. My barber of over thirty-eight years and my father's best friend was at the crusade. The Lord had me sit in front of him and his family and pray for him during the service. As Freddy Gage (deceased) was giving the invitation and inviting those who needed Jesus in their lives to come forward, the Spirit of God told me to go get him.

I walked up four flights of stairs, put my arm around him, and said to him, "L. A. McCullum, my father, who was your best friend, is in heaven with Jesus, and you know you need Jesus to forgive you and to save you. Don't you want to go to Heaven to be with my father and me because you know you need Jesus?"

He said, "Yes," and so we went together to the front for him to pray during the invitation. As we were going to the front of the coliseum, another man stepped down, put his arm around L.A. on the other side, and walked down to the front with us. After L.A. had prayed to receive Jesus and I took him up to counsel him, I asked the other man who he was. He said that he had been a barber with L.A. for over ten years and had been praying that L.A. would go to the crusade and get saved. He told the Lord that if L.A. made a decision to follow Jesus, he was going with him to the front. So, Jesus honored his prayers, and he went as a brother in Christ, rejoicing in the Lord and His grace. What was unique about this experience was the fact that two practicing Mormons had come into the coliseum and went to the top to sit. A sister in Christ came to me and told me that she thought I needed to go up there to maybe lead them to Christ. With L.A. still on my heart and mind, I asked the Lord, "If those two gentlemen are here for the show, would you please have them get up and leave, and I will go back down and sit in front of L.A.," and that is exactly what the Lord did.

I went back downstairs to sit in front of L.A., and as the Lord would speak to my heart, I would be obedient to His direction. Now prior to the crusade meeting starting that night, I had just walked into the back of the coliseum, and an older couple was sitting there. For quite a while during this time of my life, I believed that my Father God was calling me to full-time service to Him. I was sold out to Him to do His will for my life, and I told Him that if that was His will for me I had to know for sure. My first wife and children had left me because of the change in my life, so except for Jesus and my Christian family of Long Leaf, I was all alone. One Sunday night, after Sunday-night worship, God sent Pastor Larry Zaky to talk to me about God's call for my life. He testified that as he tried to bargain with God over his call to ministry for God to get him out of personal debt and sell his truck, and then he would go. Larry said that in less than two weeks, God had taken him out of $88,000 in debt. He told God that he knew that God was serious so he resigned his job and began preparing to serve God at Gardner-Webb College in Boiling Springs, North Carolina. He looked at me and said, "Jack, you said yes to God saving you so why can you not say yes to His call on your life?"

After Pastor Larry left, I got on my knees and talked to my Heavenly Father. I asked Him as I prayed, "Not my will but your will for my life is what I want to do. So if this is your will, then I say yes to it." I also told Him that I thought that I was too old to serve Him, and He showed me Moses, Abraham, and others who were older than I was when He called them to go and they went.

Father God was asking me to step out in faith and trust and obey Him. I only partially surrendered to God's call on my life at this time, but God proceeded to put the hounds of heaven on my life through His Word and continued to chase me until I totally surrendered, which took place on October 15, 1985, in Long Leaf Baptist Church in Wilmington, North Carolina. I submitted to His call on my life. I began to pray and listen to the message of God through His Word (Matthew

28:18–20 NKJV and Isaiah 6:8 NKJV). I would say in my heart as Isaiah said, "Here am I. Send me," but I also gave Him excuses as to why I could not go yet. Like many called men of God, I tried to bargain with God until I totally said yes to Him. This total surrender finally took place after Long Leaf's fall revival in October of 1985. Led by Dr. Fred Wolf (deceased) every service was Spirit-led and Spirit-filled. Every service was concluded with the hymn "I Surrender All" during invitation time, and I would hold on to the pew in front of me as the Spirit of God was encouraging me to yield totally to His call on my life.

Every night after I went home, I could not sleep, so I would go into the living room and turn on the television to hear different pastors preaching from the Word of God. Each pastor was preaching from Matthew 6:24 (NKJV): "No one can serve two masters; For either he will hate the one and love the other, or else he will be loyal to the one and despise the other. You cannot serve God and mammon," and I would weep because of the excuses and the various things I was saying to God about why I could not go to serve Him now. I was broken in spirit when I went to worship on the Sunday after the five nights of wrestling with God over my call for the rest of my life. Pastor Johnny was preaching on Matthew 6:24 (NKJV) about why we could not serve two masters. If Jesus was my Lord and Master, he said, then I must totally yield to His will for my life! My spirit broke because I understood that if He is Lord of my life, then I must trust and obey Him with the rest of my life. Therefore, I decided then in my spirit and with my will that I was going to follow Him with the rest of my life. I asked Him to lead me to the best place for me to prepare to serve Him as the best servant that I could be.

The next day, I went to work at the paper mill, walked into the superintendent's office, and told him that I was resigning on January 2, 1986, to follow God's will for my life, and for the first time, I had total peace in my heart and life as I walked out of his office. It felt like a huge boulder had been lifted off of my heart and life as I got into my car to drive home. With a time of praise, thanksgiving, and peace, I went home with joy in my spirit.

When I got home, however, there was a notice on my front door from the Wilmington, North Carolina, Police Department that they had a warrant for my arrest and to please come to the police department and straighten this out. Wow! I had never been arrested before! I began to pray for help from my Heavenly Father as I went down to the police department. I asked the Lord if they put me in jail, would He have them put me in the cell with a coworker I had been trying to share Jesus with who had been arrested and was in jail at the time?

As I walked into the police station, out walked two of my best friends. I had bowled with them in leagues at the bowling alleys in Wilmington. They came to talk to me. The lieutenant told the sergeant to take me in the back and to clear this up. When the sergeant told me to go with him to the Wilmington, North Carolina, magistrate's office, I got into the police car for the ride with him to the office. I was telling Cecil Gurganious (now deceased) what Jesus had done in my life and how I had surrendered my life to serve Him with the rest of my life. I told him that I believed that

Jesus wanted me to start at a Bible institute in the mountains of North Carolina called Fruitland Baptist Bible Institute in Fruitland, North Carolina. I told him that I was going there to enroll even though I did not have an application filled out for the school yet.

After I signed an agreement to appear in the New Hanover District Court on November 25, 1985, in Wilmington, North Carolina, we went back to the police car for the ride back to the police station. I was asked, "How much money do you have on you?" I told the officer that I had five dollars, my checkbook, and my Bible if I was put into jail. He told me that Almighty God had protected me that day because it would have cost me over $600.00 to have stayed out of jail. Now I could not understand why I had to stand in front of man for a charge that I was not guilty of, so I prayed and prayed about this matter. Finally, I heard a Christian friend who was a prayer warrior tell me that this would be a divine appointment for me. I still could not comprehend why I had to go to court, but I just trusted God was going to show me.

Before going to court for the divine appointment that I had there, I had a tumor come on my left leg that was the size of my fist. I had delayed going to the doctor with my problem with my leg. I went into the sanctuary of Long Leaf Baptist Church on Sunday to pray with six other believers for the worship service, for Pastor Johnny Hunt to have freedom to preach God's Word and for the freedom of the Holy Spirit to move in the people who were there to draw them to the Father.

After five other folks beside me had finished praying, a precious saint of God not only prayed for the pastor, for the message of God, and for the Holy Spirit of God to move in the service, but she also talked to God about my leg. She asked God to take the tumor and to heal my leg without me having to see the doctor about my problem. Well, glory to God, He took it off, and it has never come back! What a Savior! What a miracle! The closer to the date that I was to appear in court in November of 1985, the more prayers went up on my behalf from my Christian family. As I went to court on that day, I was afraid, but I knew that Jesus was still Lord, and He promised me that He would never leave me nor forsake me according to Hebrews 13:5–6 (NKJV).

While I was sitting and waiting for my case to be called, I saw a couple who had known me from the bowling alley and had watched me go through the time when Jesus was breaking me in order to save me. For over three hours, I shared what had happened to me and how Jesus had saved me and made me into a new creation with Him as my Lord. I never had to stand in front of man, because my accuser had not shown up and the district attorney dismissed my case. I could not understand why my Lord had me there at that time until the following Sunday after the time in the courtroom. I had volunteered to help answer the phones of Long Leaf's television program broadcast in the area of Wilmington, North Carolina, and across the southern areas of North and South Carolina. I was talking to Pastor Johnny Hunt, and Joe Manning (now deceased) was answering the telephones.

A mother called the number listed on the screen of the program, and Joe Manning answered it. She told Joe that she wanted to know who the man was in the courtroom of New Hanover's

Courthouse the past Tuesday. She said that she had prayed for her son and his family for fifteen years to come to church with her, and they were coming to Long Leaf Baptist Church with her that morning. Pastor Johnny asked those deacons who would be praying in the prayer room that morning to pray for them to be forgiven and saved by our Lord Jesus Christ during the service. The choir also prayed for them to be drawn to Jesus by the Holy Spirit, but they did not respond at this time.

After the benediction by Pastor Johnny, I went to them before they left that morning and invited them to come back that night to worship Jesus with the congregation. When Pastor Johnny gave the invitation that night to come to Jesus, the wife went forward to pray the sinner's prayer for Jesus to forgive her sins and to save her. She became a follower of our Lord Jesus Christ that day, but her husband did not. This personal decision of the wife was the reason that I was in the courtroom to share Jesus with that family. In addition, the miracle that took place during this time besides the new believer in Christ was that the date on this arrest warrant was October of 1984 (I was a lost unbeliever in Christ), but it was not served on me until October of 1985 after I had become a believer and follower of the Lord Jesus Christ. Now some folks would call that a coincidence, but I know that was a divine appointment for me to share my faith story with that family.

December of 1985 was awesome. It was a very precious time with me as a member of the Long Leaf choir. We were preparing to do a Christmas cantata and drama. I would be singing in the choir this time. It would be the first cantata that I would be singing in after being born again in the one the year before. It was an emotional time for me while I was singing because I kept remembering what had happened in my life the year before. It was also a special time because every time that I would sing in a choir during a Christmas and Easter cantata each year after I was saved, I would ask Christ to save someone like me who was a sinner in need of forgiveness and God's grace. I would ask the Father to save someone through His son, Jesus Christ. I also had made an application to Fruitland Baptist Bible Institute, and I was accepted by them to begin the next quarter of study on January 6, 1986.

What a joyful Christmas it was for me! I have celebrated the reason for the season every Christmas since I was saved by faith in Jesus Christ. The birth of our Lord and Savior Jesus Christ was and is awesome; however, He was born to die for the sin of all mankind. I am so grateful and thankful that He did not stay in the grave but was physically resurrected and lives again at the right hand of the Father. He is also coming again to get His church and defeat the devil for all eternity as He rules and reigns as King of kings and Lord of lords. December 1985 was also a time of preparing to begin my journey in answer to God's call on my life and to say goodbye to forty-three years of doing and living my will in Wilmington and Morehead City, North Carolina.

January of 1986 began with God closing the door on where I thought I could live for me to live on campus in a dorm of Fruitland Baptist Institute.

CHAPTER 2

Since I was a new Christian of a little over one year, my Lord knew that I needed to live in a Spirit-filled place where I could be mentored by my teachers and fellow students. It was here that I would and could grow in my faith daily as Jehovah God would soon teach me. Why? Because His plan and His will for my life had brought me this far, and in my life and will, I was being taught to trust and to obey Jesus as Lord. This school that was designed by our Lord to help those who are called by God later in life was where I needed to be. This God-ordained school with its Spirit-filled and Spirit-led teachers, most of whom were pastors or retired pastors, was where I would learn all areas of ministry that would help me to be the best servant of a Holy God that I could be.

I learned first that unless you are called of God and not mother-called, grandmother-called, or volunteered to learn a vocation, you would not be happy in your life there. The first quarter would help everyone there to settle with our Heavenly Father and His call on our lives the real reason why we were there. This group of twenty-one men and women would see only nine finish two years later for many reasons. However, these folk and the men there with us in other groups would be encouragers, prayer warriors, brothers in Christ, and fellow servants of our Lord Jesus Christ as we studied and worshiped our Lord Jesus Christ together. I made friendships with students and teachers that would help each one there grow in Christ and His call and will for our lives.

In the dorm where many of us lived, there were services held every Tuesday through Thursday night, where each called-of-God man could preach, testify, sing, pray, and worship a Holy God. God taught me here in Fruitland to never say no to Him when asked to preach, to share His Holy Word, or to testify of the grace and wonder of God in my life. God has something great to say anytime because He is the preacher. We need to remember that He just needs a vessel through whom He can preach.

Whenever I preach or testify, I ask God to speak, "Thus saith the Lord," as I stand in His Holy area to teach His Holy Word. In addition, I have learned to ask God to bind the evil one and any divisive spirit that would be present in order for the Spirit of God to speak freely through me. It was also during these worship services that I grew in wisdom and knowledge of the Word of God as the Spirit of God would teach me. Classes led by such men of God as Dr. Bill Willingham, Dr. John Rymer, Dr. Kenneth Rydings, Dr. Thad Dowdell, Dr. Ronnie Owens, and Dr. John Knight, who are all now deceased, and many others would fill my spirit and mind with God-anointed teaching and preaching on every subject important to a called man of God.

Every day in chapel worship services, we would hear a Word from God from some of the greatest preachers, teachers, and students that I have ever experienced in over twenty-eight years of ministry. The students would stand to sing praises to God, and when I would hear and sing, it would well up in me to overflow in joy and thanksgiving because of the blessings God had given to me. Every student learned about text-based expository preaching, which to me is the only way to expound on and teach people the Word of God. All the important elements in outlining Scripture and using it to explain Scripture helped me to study God's Word and become the most effective expository preacher and teacher that I could be. I learned church history, Christian counseling, Christian ethics, and the books of the Old and New Testaments. I studied the four gospels, the teachings of Jesus, and the writings of the Apostle Paul through the leadership and guidance of the Spirit of God. All of these subjects were new to a born-again former Jehovah's Witness because the Holy Spirit of God was putting in the truth the right way. It wasn't long before God would open the door for me to go to many Southern Baptist churches to share my testimony and teach about what Jehovah's Witnesses believe in order to share Christ with them. The two years I was at Fruitland, I was able to share my story in a multitude of churches and watch Jesus save people during invitation time.

After a couple of months at Fruitland, my money began to get low so I went to plan B. I soon found out that God's plan A had not stopped and He did not need any help from me to provide for me. He let me have a little job as a waiter in a Christian restaurant in Chimney Rock, North Carolina, to teach me to trust Him. Even though I led an over-the-road truck driver to saving faith in Jesus Christ the first night I worked, it began to take me away from my studies and my calling from God. Soon I thanked the owners for giving me a job, but I knew in my heart that I had run ahead of God instead of trusting Him so I stopped working there. This became a faith lesson for me, as He was growing my faith.

The next lesson of faith came when the fourteenth day of a fifteen-day grace period for insurance came due on God's car that He let me have, and I had no money. Many times, I had told God of my need, and I asked Him that if He did not provide the money to send people to take me where I needed to go. As I was standing outside of the dorm crying out to God over my need, Rick Phillips drove up in his truck and parked in the parking lot of the dorm. He got out, walked up to me, and said, "You have a need that God said that I was to help to meet, so what is it? And don't you lie to me."

I began to tear up because only God knew my need, and I knew in my heart that He had sent Rick to help me. I told Rick about the money due for the insurance on the car. Rick told me to come with him, and we drove to the local post office to send the money by registered mail so it would be there by the deadline that it was due. Another faith answer for me to trust God more was delivered through the Holy Spirit and Rick Phillips to me! In addition, when we got back to the dorm rooms and Rick went to his room, on his desk was the money that he had paid for my bill plus more than that from God. Rick and I both learned a great faith lesson because we could not outgive a Holy God who loves His children and promises to take care of their needs if they seek His kingdom first.

A few weeks went by after this faith lesson by my Lord before He would teach me another lesson to grow my faith. My car—forgive me, God's car—broke down and had to be towed to the garage for repairs. As I was standing beside the car on the shoulder of the road waiting for the local mechanic I had called, a carload of Baptist preachers from Fruitland who had been to Hendersonville, North Carolina, on a shopping trip saw me and stopped to check on me. They knew that I had been invited to a Southern Baptist Church in Brevard, North Carolina, to share my story with the youth and adults of that church. The driver said that He would take me as soon as he took the other men to the dorm rooms. He stopped at the garage and picked me up to travel to the Baptist church in Brevard. After I had shared my testimony and my faith with these folks and answered their questions about the Watchtower Society, two young adults committed their lives by faith in Jesus Christ as their Lord and Savior during the commitment and invitation time. After this experience, the Lord confirmed in my heart and spirit that He is Lord and when I go in His name, He will provide the way for me. I began to seek where the Lord would have me serve Him after visiting many local Southern Baptist churches near Fruitland Baptist Institute. He made it very clear to me that I was to serve Him in Hickory, North Carolina, in Penelope Baptist Church, which I will talk about later in this story. The Lord used my roommate, Dr. Steve Parker, to tell me where he believed God wanted me to serve Him while I was preparing to serve Him with my life and ministries. When I went to sleep praying for God to give me a clear direction as to where He wanted me to serve Him, I began to see Preacher Parker standing and preaching to me God's will and direction for my life was to serve Him in Penelope Baptist Church. I heard Him say to my heart that He wanted one person sold out to Him to become a member and minister to them. I said yes to His will and call on my life to serve Him in Penelope Baptist Church. This was also the home church of my uncle Ray Harwell and my aunt Wilma Harwell, with whom I was staying on the weekends. I would also stay with my aunt Mildred Kincaid in Granite Falls, North Carolina, some of my cousins, and my aunt Betty Carter. Two of my aunts, Wilma and Betty (both deceased), had lost sons to death, and it was as if our Lord had given them a son to love and to help as he prepared for the ministry. When I needed new shoes and a college dictionary, my aunt Betty gave me a new pair of penny loafers and a college dictionary that had belonged to her son Wayne, who was with the Lord. She also let me sleep in his bed when I would stay with her. Uncle Ray and Aunt Wilma (both deceased) would feed me and give me money for my needs. Aunt Mildred (deceased) also gave me a bed to sleep in and fed me wonderful meals. She would pray for me every day.

God used my family to take care of me as I served Him with my life. They were so happy that I was born again and that I had said yes to God's call on my life to serve Him with the rest of my life. For them to have a Baptist preacher and evangelist in their family was an awesome experience, and helping me prepare for the ministry brought joy and a blessing to their lives. I was single again because my first wife had abandoned me and filed for divorce. I was against the divorce, but she had free will to divorce me. God showed me that He never forces His will on anybody so the divorce went through. Even though my heart was broken over my wife rejecting me, I still cared for her with all of my heart. Under spiritual advice from Dr. John Rymer, I went to the divorce proceedings in May of 1986 to stop the divorce and to give God's stand on divorce, which was my belief also. This would be a sad day for me, but God's grace got me through this as He allowed every decision my wife of almost twenty-two years would make. I sat in the courtroom and waited for the judge to call our case. I was continually praying for the Lord to stop the divorce. As our case was called and my wife went forward, a man in the courtroom stood and said, "Your Honor, I have not seen anything about this case. Would it be possible for me to review it?" The proceedings were stopped, and my wife had to sit down for a period of time to wait for the judge to call the case again. The Holy Spirit of God impressed on my heart that it was not God's will for a divorce to happen, but He would not force His will on anyone. He said that my wife must choose what she wanted with her own will and decision in life. After the judge gave her the divorce, I sat and waited to speak before the court and the judge, as I had not signed anything to agree with the divorce. Later, I was told by a lawyer that because I did not have a lawyer to represent me and had not signed the papers agreeing to it, the divorce was granted. I left the courtroom with tears in my eyes, as a woman who had been a part of my life for over twenty-two years was no longer my wife.

I had arrived in Wilmington about five days prior to that date. Joe Manning and his wife (both deceased) told me that I could stay with them during this period of time after I had called them. On Monday of that week, Joe asked me to make a visit with him to talk to a husband of a lady in the local rest home. Brother Joe and other folks from Long Leaf Baptist Church would go to that rest home to do worship services every other Sunday afternoon during this time, and he had promised this wife, who was a patient there, that he would visit her husband, who was an alcoholic and a nonbeliever in Jesus Christ. We went to his trailer but were not sure which one he lived in. A young boy on his bicycle asked us whom we were looking for and led us to the right house. We were asked in by the man, who was already drunk early on this morning. When we asked him if he knew for certain that he would be in heaven with Jesus, with tears in his eyes, he answered that he was a drunk and he knew that he was not worthy of heaven. He knew that he would be separated from God in hell because of his drinking and his sin. I told him that it was not drinking that would keep him out of Heaven but saying no to Jesus as his Lord and Savior.

I had written a funeral sermon for my Evangelism Explosion class at Fruitland using Ecclesiastes 3:1–2 (NKJV) and the evangelistic tool of Evangelism Explosion. My Lord used this to show the man his need for forgiveness of sin and to believe that Jesus is who the Bible teaches He is. He prayed from his heart the sinner's prayer and was weeping as he asked Jesus to forgive him of his sin and to save him. A new born-again believer and follower of Jesus was born of God into His family that morning! The Lord used me again the day before the divorce proceedings to once again lead a lost soul to saving faith in Jesus Christ as his Lord and Savior. This man stopped me on the street and asked me for money so he could eat. I told him that I would take him to eat but not just give him money.

While we were eating, I asked him to tell me his life's story and what was happening in his life now. I also asked him if he knew where he would spend eternity. He said that he had given his heart to Christ at the age of eight, asking him to forgive him of his sins and to save him. He said that he told God that he was a sinner and that he believed that Jesus was the Son of God, who was born of a virgin, died on a cruel cross to pay for his sins, and was resurrected in a physical resurrection. He also said that Jesus was coming again soon to get His church and to rule and reign as King of kings and Lord of lords. My spirit bore witness that he did belong to Jesus as His child, and I needed to help him. I prayed with him and gave him money and the phone numbers of some folks to call for a job. I left him that morning wondering if God had sent him to get my mind off of my problems before I went to court.

In July of 1986, I decided to go to Wilmington for my twenty-fifth high school reunion. I also was praying that my Lord would help me to speak to many of my classmates about what Jesus had done for me and His call to me to prepare to serve Him with my life. I also had some mates who were Jehovah's Witnesses, and I asked the Lord to allow me to share with them what Jesus had done for me. One of my classmates, whom I had not seen in over thirty years, was now a believer and an attorney living in Florida. Two of the students had married and moved to Atlanta, Georgia, so they would not be disfellowshipped. I shared my faith with them, but they chose to say no at that time to Jesus as their Lord and Savior. The two who sat in judgment of me did not come, so I could not speak to them.

Before I came to Wilmington, I had called my mother to ask her if I could stay with her while I was there. She had said yes, but when I returned to her house the first night of being there, all of my clothes and toiletries were in a basket on the front porch. She put a note in the basket that said that I had made my bed so I could not stay with her. Because of my decision to believe in and follow by faith Jesus Christ as my Lord and Savior, my mother could not sit with me, eat with me, or talk to me because she would be excommunicated from the Watchtower Society. This was her way of saying she did not approve of my life as a Baptist minister or my studying to be a Southern Baptist minister in the school that I was in.

In June of 1986, I began to serve as the interim minister of the youth of Penelope Baptist Church in Hickory, North Carolina, and to teach the high school age young people. The search committee was still looking to find a young man to fill the position, but they had not found the right man of God to call to serve the youth of Penelope. I also went to Ridgecrest Conference Center in Black Mountain, North Carolina, for Sunday school training with the young people in order to become the best servant of our Lord Jesus Christ to them. I would go to Fruitland for classes during the day and spend the afternoon and evening in classes at Ridgecrest. While I was there at Ridgecrest, I was able to share my testimony with the folks of many Southern Baptist churches across North Carolina, South Carolina, Tennessee, and other southern states. The Lord Jesus Christ opened up many doors of opportunity for me to preach, to share my testimony, and to teach and do seminars in churches and conferences. I was being used by my Lord in a mighty way to lead people to Him for His glory, as He would add to His kingdom. I continued to lead the youth for many months until they called a youth minister to lead them.

In late August of 1986, I was invited to share my story in a Southern Baptist church in Robbins, North Carolina, by another student in Fruitland who was a member and stayed in the dorm with me as he prepared for the ministry.

The Maness family (all deceased) invited me to come and stay in Robbins while I was there to share with their home church. The parents of a fellow student at Fruitland (now deceased) were in poor health and spent most of their income on medicine and doctors.

I spent some time in Wilmington with my Christian family from Long Leaf before going to Robbins and returning to Fruitland for my studies. In the Wednesday night worship service at Long Leaf Baptist Church in Wilmington, North Carolina, a young believer whom I had mentored and helped gave me some money because of his love for the Lord. With this extra money, God was going to answer the prayers of the mother of the Maness family. After I arrived at the their home and had seen the needs of this family, the Lord had me take the son (now deceased) to the local grocery store to buy items for them. As we would go up and down the aisles of food, whatever my Lord would say to put in the basket, we did. This even included toilet paper, and I asked the Lord, "Are you sure, toilet paper for the family?"

He said, "Yes!"

We then went back to the Maness home to take all the groceries into the house and explained to the parents that these were provided by the Lord through His children.

On the Sunday after preaching and sharing my story with the folks of their home church, the mother gave me a letter and asked me to read it whenever I had time. I stopped to get gas after leaving them, and I read the letter. The mother poured out her heart in thanksgiving to God for all the items she had received from Him—even for the toilet paper. She had been praying for these items for four days and trusting God for them, and we were used by God to meet her and the family's needs! Well glory to God for using me to help meet a praying Hannah of God!

When I returned to Fruitland, I had this family on my heart so I told Rick Phillips of the needs of the Maness family. He asked the students of Fruitland to help meet their needs. Rick told the leadership of Fruitland and the ministerial students who were there that God wanted to use us to help the Maness family. I had also told the pastor of Penelope Baptist Church, and he said to have Rick Phillips come by Penelope so the church could give him food for the family also. Rick took a car loaded down with food and money to give to the Maness family from their Christian family. This was a great experience for me, Rick, and the Maness family to see God answer the prayers of His children and to use His children to deliver the needs. I still well up in my spirit as I remember this experience! I had been sharing my story with many churches, including Penelope, and watching God grow my faith and add to His Kingdom during the months of September and October of 1986.

It was during the exam week in early October of 1986 that my Lord would bring into my life the Godly woman that I had been praying for for over three years. I had asked God to please bring into my life a woman whom He had called to be a minister's wife. (I had watched two of my roommates have to get out of the ministry because their wives did not want to be a pastor's wife.) I also prayed for a wife whom God had called into missions and who was finished with her child-bearing years, although I was willing to help raise her children if it was necessary. I believed in my heart it was necessary in order for us to serve the Lord for the rest of our lives together. I prayed for this woman of God daily. I prayed that God would meet these prayer requests and then waited on Him.

With this in mind, I was to take a New Testament and an Old Testament exam, and I needed help if I was to pass the exams that morning. I had been sick most of the night, and I was doing a lot of praying, asking God for help to remember what I needed to please Him and to pass the exams. I was sitting in the Old Testament class waiting and praying for help, when one of my fellow preacher students walked in and told me that he had a letter for me to read. I opened the letter, and in it was a card, which I took out.

On the front of this card were these words from God's Word: "Remember, God has never failed in all His promises" (2 Kings 8:56 NKJV). I opened the inside of the card and read those words from our God to my heart, and I began to weep because when I needed a Word from God, He had sent this card from Janet VanDyke. She thanked me for sharing my story with Penelope and teaching the folks about what the Watchtower Society believes so we could share Jesus with them. When I returned to Hickory on that Friday, I went to ask a precious couple in Penelope who Janet VanDyke was because I wanted to thank her. They told me that she was a greeter on the right-hand side of Penelope, and so I went that following Sunday to find her and to thank her for the letter. I did not know that it would be four Sundays later before I would meet her because of her work schedule with Kroger's Sav-On Food, and I was preaching in Concord Baptist Church in Granite Falls, North Carolina, one Sunday.

On the Sunday that I had finally met her and thanked her, her mother, Edith Rhoney, sent Janet to ask me to go to lunch with them. The Lord impressed on my heart that Janet was a Godly woman and I needed to know her more. So that night, I helped her with the toddlers of Penelope during the worship time, and we were able to learn more about each other even though I had been in Penelope for about one year.

After the service, we went with other members of Penelope to the local Shoney's for food and fellowship time. What a marvelous time I had! I believed in my heart that this lady was worth knowing better.

When I went to sleep in my dorm room after meeting Janet, God woke me up to speak to my heart about her. He began to do work for both of us as we found out later. Janet had not asked God for a preacher, just a Godly Christian man, since she was single again. I told her that I did not ask God to do this calling, nor did I volunteer for the call. I told her that God would not let me be happy doing anything else except obeying His call on my life. We would study God's Word together, and she would go with me when I was asked to churches to preach and to testify.

On December 11, 1986, I finished another quarter at Fruitland Baptist Bible Institute. I had been invited to three Baptist churches in Wilmington and Carolina Beach, North Carolina, to do their worship services. I knew in my heart as I traveled to the Wilmington area that Janet was the wife that God had sent into my life to be a partner in marriage and ministry. So when I returned Sunday night, December 13, 1986, to Penelope Baptist Church for their Senior Christmas play and musical, I went in, sat down, and asked Janet to join me. That night after the service, I asked Janet to marry me. I told her that all I had was Jesus, His car, my clothes, and myself. I had no home, no job, and no money to start this marriage. I was in school preparing to serve God with the rest of my life.

She said yes to my marriage proposal, but she also said that we could not get married yet. We prayed about the ceremony, and we both agreed on February 21, 1987, because I would have a two-week break before the next quarter at Fruitland would start. We asked Dr. Harvey Myers (deceased), who was the pastor of Penelope Baptist Church, to do the covenant marriage between Janet, myself, and God. He said yes. I also asked the men of God who were students with me to be a part of the wedding ceremony. I asked Dr. Steve Parker to pray during the ceremony; Reverend Kenny Pardue, Reverend Terry Burris, and Reverend Rick Phillips to be ushers; and my uncle Ray Harwell to be the best man. In addition to these, Brother Bob Fleming (deceased) offered to take photographs of the wedding as a wedding gift to Janet and me. They were awesome. Janet was so beautiful and still is. Janet's mother and her family provided everything for the wedding.

The reception for our marriage was awesome, especially since we did not have money. Janet bought our wedding bands and my new suit because my clothes were old and out of date and I had no money! The pastor said that I had to get married to get a place to sleep. I went from a twin-size bed to a king-size bed for a King's kid! Jehovah God blessed my life with His choice of a wife. She has brought joy and happiness into my life as we serve our Lord together. Besides Janet, the Lord also blessed me with having her mother, Edith Rhoney, in my life for many years to teach me how to pray and how to love others with God's unconditional love and compassion. In addition, her daughters, Angela VanDyke Brown and Tracy VanDyke Chapman, became my daughters. Janet received my children, Alex Ryan Burns and Angela Louise Burns, as her children. Then our Lord added grandchildren to our families.

My father, Harry Lee Burns, died and went to be with our Lord in March of 1985, and my mother, Geraldine Collins Burns, also went to be with our Lord in 2000 while Janet and I were International Mission Board missionaries of the Southern Baptist Convention serving our Lord in South Korea. God sure blessed our lives with our families. It was during this time in Penelope that I grew in the Lord as God was showing me how to serve Him in any area where He would use me. I sang in the choir of Penelope, which also gave me the opportunity to sing in the Christmas and Easter cantatas and to remind the church that I was saved during the musicals and dramas.

Therefore, we would pray that the Holy Spirit of God would draw to the Father those who would hear the voice of our Lord Jesus Christ as we sang the gospel during the service. I have heard that other folks would listen to the message in the songs during these special worship times and commit their lives by faith in the Lord Jesus Christ, becoming believers and followers of Jesus. I personally experienced this, and it happened in later years when we were International Mission Board missionaries in Brazil and South Africa. I also began to teach a Bible Sunday school class with the adults after Penelope called a youth pastor. I named my class "Pairs, Spares, and I Don't Care." I would study so I could preach and teach the Word of God. This would help me to be a real servant of God's Word.

I studied both at Fruitland and in personal devotion time. I also continued to share my story and teach on the witnesses in other Southern Baptist churches and in school. In May of 1987, Fruitland Baptist Institute celebrated "Founders' Days," which they did yearly in the month of May. Our wives were also asked to join in the celebration time. They would have their meetings of worship and study while their husbands were in class in the mornings. We would come together to hear great preaching after lunch by great Southern Baptist Pastors and Evangelists from great churches around the Southern Baptist convention for two days.

Before Janet and I traveled to Fruitland for Founders' Days in May of 1987, we helped our youngest daughter, Tracy, to trust by faith in Jesus Christ, which stirred our hearts because we knew that we would be together in heaven with Jesus. She had been in our hearts, and the Holy Spirit of God had her ready to say yes to Jesus when we led her in the sinner's prayer to saving faith in Jesus. This was an awesome time in our lives, as our Lord was leading us to share our stories with people of all denominations and our families and watch Him change lives for His glory. We were able to take three of our grandsons with us to Penelope Baptist Church in Hickory, North Carolina, so they could hear the Word of God and also go to Sunday School and to teach them God's Holy Word personally.

Janet and I could teach and live out God's Word during their young years. We would also take them with us when we were invited to other Baptist churches to share our stories so they could understand that the family of God was in other churches also. They would enjoy this time because many of these Baptist Churches had dinner on the grounds.

I then began to hear and to feel that my Lord was asking me to go further in my preparation to serve Him after my time at Fruitland. I prayed and sought God's will for my life. I asked if I should go and where. I prayed that if He was serious about me going further in my education He would have one of my teachers at Fruitland tell me. At the bottom of one of my test papers in Dr. John Knight's (deceased) class, he wrote that he felt led by the Holy Spirit to tell me that God wanted me to go further in my preparation to serve Him with my life. Well, there it was!

CHAPTER 3

I had to begin to pray as to the school He wanted me to attend. I asked that He would please help me since I was new in my marriage. I knew that Jesus was first in my life, but as He designed it, Janet was next in my life and ministry. When I told Janet that God had told me to go further in my preparation, she did not say anything. We both prayed about this over the next couple of months and came to the conclusion that God was leading me to Gardner-Webb University (Proverbs 16:3, 9 NKJV). I applied and was accepted as a student in their bachelor of arts in religious studies.

After four months of study to complete my associate divinity degree in Fruitland Baptist Bible Institute in December of 1987, I would begin the next chapter of my life starting in January of 1988. God would use me as a preacher in the chapel services of Fruitland and in many ways for His glory during these four months.

One very special experience at the First Baptist Church of Cherryville, North Carolina, happened at a Sunday night worship service. I was teaching the congregation about how to share their personal salvation story with Jehovah's Witnesses. After the invitation and benediction, I went to the vestibule, and Pastor Mike Minnex (now deceased) introduced me to an unshaven and dirty man. Pastor Mike told me that the man was hitchhiking from Ohio to Greenville, South Carolina, to find work and a place to stay. Pastor Mike had called the Salvation Army in Gastonia, North Carolina, to find the man a place to sleep for the night plus meals until he left for Greenville.

The Lord impressed on my heart to tell the man that I could come and pick him up to take him to Greenville, South Carolina, on my way back to Fruitland that Monday. (Monday was traveling day for the students of Fruitland.) I went to Gastonia to get the man for his ride to Greenville and to help him find a Southern Baptist church there that would help him find a job and a place to stay.

As we were traveling, I told him that this was the Lord's car that we were riding in (a 1982 Honda Prelude), and whoever was riding in the car, I always asked where he or she stood with his or her relationship to Jesus Christ.

The man said, "I know Him personally, but I am here to talk to you about your mother!"

I asked him how he knew my mother. I had been praying for over two years for her salvation, and she would not talk to me because of the threat of being disfellowshipped by the Jehovah's Witnesses. He told me all about my mother and her relationship with Jesus, and I was having a hard time believing and comprehending what he was saying. We fell silent before arriving in Greenville, South Carolina at a Southern Baptist Church.

The angel of the Lord spoke to Hagar in Genesis 16:7–8 (NKJV):

> Now the Angel of the Lord found her (Hagar) by the spring of water in the wilderness, by the spring on the way to Shur. And He said, "Hagar, Sarai's maid, where have you come from, and where are you going? She said, "I am fleeing from the presence of my mistress Sarai."

In addition, in Exodus 23:20 (NKJV), we read, "Behold, I send an Angel before you to keep you in the way and to bring you into the place which I have prepared." In Numbers 22:23 (NKJV), the Bible says, "Then God's anger was aroused because he went, and the Angel of the Lord took His stand in the way as an adversary against him. And he was riding on his donkey, and his two servants were with him."

There are thirty-two examples in the Bible where the angel of the Lord appeared to people, and I do believe that I had an angel of the Lord in my car riding with me! I pulled into the parking lot next to the doors to the office, and I told the man to go into the office, and the people there would help him find a job and a place to stay. He got out of the car, and I waited to see him go into the office, but I never saw him go into the office.

Soon, I got out of my car to see where he had gone, but he had disappeared! I began to wonder what had happened to him. I asked the Lord, "Where did he go?" I then asked, "Did You send him?" Was the man one of His angels that He, the Lord, had sent to talk to me? I had read about this happening to others, but I had never had it happen to me before. I began to radiate as if I had just received four thousand volts of His electricity through my body. I told Him that I understood that He had sent the man, but the next day, I would understand more fully about this time when I received a phone call from my mother in the dorm where I was staying. My mother was not happy about my decision to follow Jesus with my life, and she had told me so many times. But for her to call me in the dorm of that Baptist school was to be a miracle in my life and heart. I had grieved over her salvation as I prayed every day for Jesus to lift the blinders the evil one had put over her eyes and heart and to save her. As she was talking to me, she said that she had had a personal encounter with the Lord Jehovah Jesus Christ when she was young! My heart was full of joy and thanksgiving after I asked her to explain what she meant by this statement. She answered me by saying that when she was nine years old, she had asked Jesus Christ into her heart and to forgive her and save her! I held the phone away from my head and shouted, "Well, glory to God! My mother is born again!"

The students in the dorm rooms came out into the hall, and I shouted very loudly that my mother was a born-again follower of Jesus Christ and that we would be together forever! I then called Janet to tell her the good news about my mother, and she shared the miracle with the folks of Penelope, as they had been praying for her salvation also. That week in Fruitland was a joy and a blessing. I shared in chapel about my mother's born-again experience, and we all rejoiced in the Lord. I also enjoyed preaching in my class before my peers and teachers and being critiqued for my sermon. Dr. George Lockabee (deceased) and Dr. Kenneth Ridings (deceased) would tape our sermons for us to see ourselves and to understand how and why we were critiqued to help us improve. I really thank the Lord that they would give to each preacher an outline on the passage that we preached to help us to see the division of Scripture, to decide the theme of the passage of Scriptures that we were preaching on, to do expository text-based preaching with, and to show us how to outline the Word of God. This would be my way of preparing and preaching, "thus saith the Lord," wherever I was preaching for my Lord in His Holy area for over twenty-five years.

In the latter months of my experience at Fruitland, I developed friendships with many of the students and teachers that would continue throughout my life. Therefore, the study time, the class time, the worship time in the chapel of Fruitland, the wonderful food served in the cafeteria (I gained about twenty pounds while living there), the fellowship time with students and teachers, and all of the experiences that I had while there at Fruitland helped me to grow in faith and in my relationship with my Lord Jesus Christ. Many of the great sermon topics I learned as they would be preached to my heart at Fruitland would be used by the Holy Spirit of God later in my life. As I would preach many of these passages for my Lord, I was amazed at what He would recall. He wanted to teach me that as He had revealed His Word to those servants, the same Holy Spirit would help me that day and every day as the teacher.

In a special Sunday morning worship service on October 4, 1987, at Penelope Baptist Church, led by Dr. Harvey Myers, the congregation licensed me to the Gospel ministry. The folks of Penelope had watched my life as I was serving God and His call on my life, and many testified on my behalf. I was both honored and blessed by my Christian family of Penelope, as they were also used to cover my expenses for over a year while I was studying at Fruitland Baptist Bible Institute. There was a scholarship available for any member who was called by God into His service, and they said that I qualified as a member of Penelope. They prayed for us and our ministries, helped meet the needs of Janet and me through love gifts, and loved and encouraged us each time that we met to worship.

Janet had grown up in that fellowship of believers and had been saved at eight and a half years old. She went through all the mission classes for girls and had been on a mission to West Virginia to help plant and start a new Baptist work in Wheeling, West Virginia. She had a call to missions when she was young but never knew that God would put a preacher in her life and remind her of that call for service as my wife. Our Lord put her and her mother, Edith Rhoney, in my life to teach me how to pray and to pray believing aaccording to Mark 11:24 (NKJV).

God also put Janet in my life to help me to know that I needed to start the day with the Lord in prayer, Bible reading, and devotion time. She would rise at 3:30 a.m. each morning before she worked at Kroger's to do her prayer time and devotion time, using *Open Windows*, a Southern Baptist devotion book, and *In Touch* from First Baptist in Atlanta, Georgia. She would also read Sunday school material from Lifeway, an education provider for Southern Baptist churches. Instead of waiting to study and read at night when I could not stay awake but fell asleep, I began to get up early and start the day with the Lord. She also played the piano before the opening assembly of the seniors' Sunday school classes in Penelope, and she would use this talent in our ministries for many years. Janet was and is my helpmate in marriage and in ministry, and the Lord blessed my life by putting her in my life as my life mate.

November went by quickly as Janet and I celebrated our first Thanksgiving together with our families and a community Thanksgiving service of evangelical churches in Bethany Lutheran Church in Hickory, North Carolina.

December came, and with it came my graduation from Fruitland Baptist Bible Institute and our first celebration of Christmas as a family. We both sang in the Christmas cantata at Penelope, and it was a spirit-filled time worshiping Jesus, who is the reason for this time of the year. I said goodbye to many of the students God had put into my life during this time of instruction and faith, growing by my Lord Jesus Christ. The wives of those who were graduating, including Janet, received a PHT diploma, which means "putting husband through," to recognize their help and their support for their husbands in this ministry preparation time.

Before I conclude the experiences of 1987 in my life, I must relate a true experience in leading a lady to saving faith in Jesus Christ. Janet had called me in the dorm to tell me that a lady in Penelope wanted to see me and talk to me about her relationship with Jesus Christ. I told Janet to tell her that as soon as I returned to Hickory Janet and I would visit her in her home.

Janet and I arrived at her home that Friday afternoon to hear this lady tell us that she was going to the local hospital for surgery the next day, and she was worried about her soul and where she would spend eternity. She told us that when she was young and attending a revival meeting, she had gone forward with some of her friends when the evangelist gave an invitation to come to Jesus. She really had no peace in her heart that she was born again, so she asked us to help her make sure that she was saved based on God's Word. I asked her if she would pray the same prayer that Janet and I did from her heart to Jesus. I told her that He would forgive her and save her. She got on her knees with Janet and me, and I led her in the sinner's prayer. She began to weep as she confessed to Jesus that she was a sinner and could not save herself. She told Jesus that she believed that He was the Son of God, that He was born into this world, that He died for her sins on the cross, and that He was resurrected in a physical resurrection and was coming back to rule and reign as King of kings and Lord of lords. She then thanked Jesus for forgiving her sins and saving her.

When she got up weeping, I showed her that based on the Word of God in Romans 10:9–13 and 1 John 5: 9–13 (NKJV), she was now a born-again follower of Jesus Christ and would be with Him for all eternity! She also had now become one of God's family based on John 1:12–13 (NKJV) as a child of God. Before we left, after hugging her and telling her that we were her sister and brother in Christ, I asked her if she now had peace in her heart concerning where she would spend eternity. She answered us with a resounding yes! Why? Because Jesus had settled in her heart that He was her Lord and she was His child! Wow, a new child of Jesus! His kingdom was now a witness of His saving grace and would testify to what He had settled in her heart and life. She went through the surgery, resting in Jesus, and came out fine. She continues to this day as a witness to God's grace and glory!

The year of 1987 would be an awesome year in my life because He brought the wife that I had prayed for over three years together with me in a covenant marriage! I had finished the first chapter in my life at Fruitland Baptist Bible Institute in preparation to become the best servant of our Lord. I had watched God grow my faith so that I could trust and obey Him more. I had also been able to share my story of God's grace given to me through faith in Jesus Christ as my Lord and Savior with many folks! I watched the Holy Spirit of God draw many to the Father in saving faith through belief in Jesus Christ as their Lord and Savior, especially our youngest daughter, Tracy, as I would give an invitation! God sure is good all the time, and He is faithful to His Word!

I now had a Christian family in the folks of Penelope Baptist Church, who would pray and support us and our ministries. God had also given me a family, which seemed to have been taken away from me when I became a believer and follower of Jesus Christ! I was excited about the future because God had given me Jeremiah 29:11 (NKJV) as assurance in my life.

CHAPTER 4

The year 1988 would become a new chapter in my life from my Lord, and I was excited to see and to hear all that He would do in my life during my time at Gardner-Webb University! As I began the process in the first part of January of 1988 to enter Gardner-Webb University as a student in their bachelor of arts in religious studies, I met with the folks who were processing my application. I also met with those who were over the financial aid department. They told me that there would be foundations that would put money into my education along with the individual Southern Baptist churches' gifts of money. Since I was commuting five days a week from Hickory, North Carolina, to the campus of Gardner-Webb in Boiling Springs, North Carolina, the aid department also sent money to the religion department, which would also provide aid for me every semester. God sure took care of my needs!

I had found out that Gardner-Webb was only giving me credit for thirty-two hours' transfer from Fruitland Baptist Bible Institute into my major, and I was disappointed with this decision. I soon was told that if I went to the University of North Carolina at Asheville in Asheville, North Carolina, and took a test given to folks of my age, because I was forty-five years old, Gardner-Webb would give me more credit hours to apply to my time.

As I was driving to Asheville, North Carolina, the Holy Spirit of the Lord impressed on my heart this question: "Where are you going, Jack? There is no shortcut in doing what I have called you to do!" I immediately turned around and went back home because this was of me and not God. I remembered once more that He leads and I follow. I knew that that decision was all mine and not His for my life.

I was introduced to a young vision-impaired student from the Hickory, North Carolina, area by the financial aid department, and I was asked if I could let him ride with me to and from the Gardner-Webb campus. I said yes and was told that the state of North Carolina would pay for all of my gas expenses while we were commuting to the campus. I soon found out that the young man was a believer and follower of Jesus Christ, and he would ask a lot of theological and biblical questions for me to answer. There were many times when I did not know the answers, but I told him that I would study and find out for him. He kept me on my toes and in God's Word many days, which helped me to know the answers.

I asked Dr. R. Logan Carson (now deceased), one of the Old Testament professors and a man of God, to be my advisor to help me to fulfill the requirements in my major as well as my minor, which was social psychology. He became a mentor. He was a wonderful professor in the Old Testament area of study and an advisor to help me to fulfill all of the requirements for a bachelor of arts in religious studies with a minor in social psychology. I have also come to trust my Lord Jesus Christ and His Words of instruction in Proverbs 16:3, 9 (NKJV): "Commit your works to the Lord, And your thoughts will be established ... A man's heart plans his way, But the Lord directs his steps." I will always pray for God's will and direction for my life to have control instead of trusting in my feelings.

I was excited but scared when I signed up for my first classes at Gardner-Webb University on that day in January of 1988. I would soon find out when I went to the different classes for the first time that I was older than all my teachers except one. The other students liked it because they had a fellow student who had lived during the 1940s, the 1950s, the 1960s, and the 1970s to the day that I came to Gardner-Webb. While there preparing to serve God in ministry, I became the father and grandfather to many of the students on campus. I had been out of high school for over twenty-five years, and I was there because of God's call for my life to prepare to be the best servant of His that I could become.

The first semester went by fast, but I began to learn about different ideas and thoughts on many different liberal art studies, which I would use in the future. My teachers were wonderful. Many liked me being in their class so that I could give an older person's view and thoughts on the different subjects. I had also become a member of the Ministerial Alliance of Gardner-Webb along with twenty three other preachers, and the campus minister would assign all twenty-three of us to different Southern Baptist churches over the western area of North Carolina to practice preaching and to be critiqued by the different pastors. Janet would also go with me, and on many occasions, God would use her to play the piano for the services.

Soon, the summer break came. I had asked God to give me a place of service that I could serve Him in. Penelope's day care director asked me to come to meet with her. There, I would find out God's assignment for the summer of 1988 for me. It would not be what I thought but what God wanted me to do. Janet told me that Penelope's day care was looking for a man to drive their day care bus, and I should go talk to the director. I went to the day care, and while I was sitting outside the director's office, I overheard the director and assistant director saying that they had prayed for a man to drive the bus. This man would drive the seventy-five plus students and teachers to their various places during the summer. The Holy Spirit of God impressed on my heart, "Jack, you will be that man to serve them as the driver!" I could not believe that God wanted me to haul seventy-five screaming children every day during the week to the places the director had for them to go. What a lesson of obedience I would receive in what would seem a small assignment for God!

During the second or third time I took the children to one of the local pools near Penelope Baptist Church in the Longview area of Hickory, North Carolina, I led one of the lifeguards to saving faith in Jesus Christ as her personal Lord and Savior. I had shared with her a couple of times about what Jesus Christ had done for me and what He would do for her. She believed in Jesus and was forgiven of her sins, and she became a born-again follower of Jesus Christ! I knew then why God had me drive the bus.

Another great experience would happen about a month later while the children were eating lunch in the cafeteria of the day care. A man who was homeless and hungry came into the day care, and I asked the cooks to help him by giving him lunch to eat, which they did. After he had eaten, I took him into the sanctuary of Penelope Baptist Church, and I led him to faith in Jesus Christ as his personal Lord and Savior on the altar. He told me that nobody had shown him hospitality and love like the folks of Penelope Day Care. We then called the local Salvation Army in Hickory, North Carolina, and they gave the man a place to stay that included meals. They also said that they would help him find a job. All this experience made me say in my heart, *Well, glory to God!*

As I registered for the New Year at Gardner-Webb, I chose the classes that Dr. Carson and my Lord chose for me to grow in Christ. First, I began the two-year study of Biblical Greek during this semester, which would prove to be awe inspiring. I studied the original language of the New Testament. The Holy Spirit would teach me His Word as He did the writers of the New Testament.

Every class that I took would help me to be the best servant that I could be as I served my Lord. I was grateful for every teacher who helped me to become that servant. The classes in English helped me to learn new words and how to read literature and write papers for my classes. The sociology and psychology classes would help me to minister to the needs of others as well as understand myself better. Even the history classes were great, as I studied the past and the future up to that time. I became interested in the history of World War II because many of my family had served in that great war. I read many books and watched many movies about this time. I agree with many folks that this was the greatest generation of the history of the United States.

I was one of the visiting preaching students sent from Gardner-Webb to local Southern Baptist churches in North Carolina. In addition, I was invited to the churches of some of my fellow students to share my story and to teach the folks what Jehovah's Witnesses believe and trust in so they could share the gospel of Jesus Christ. During this time, I was invited to an Evangelical Methodist church in Drexel, North Carolina, to share my story and to teach the folks about the beliefs and practices of the Watchtower Society of Jehovah's Witnesses. During the invitation time, seven people recognized their need to confess to Jesus that they were sinners and asked Him to forgive them and to save them and become their personal Lord and Savior. Glory to God for his grace and mercy, which will save anyone who calls on Him in faith!

I also learned another lesson about judging anyone who is worshipping our Lord in faith in corporate worship time. Janet and I had gone to worship and for me to preach in a Southern Baptist church in Lenoir, North Carolina. A young lady got up to sing the special song before I preached God's Word. I thought to myself that her voice was terrible, and I asked God to heal her voice. The Spirit of God impressed on my heart, "Jack, she is singing to Me from her heart, and it sounds wonderful to Me!" I asked God to forgive me and told Him that the song sounded awesome! He was teaching me that I was not to judge anyone who was singing, testifying, or preaching for His glory!

Another lesson that I have learned since Jesus saved me is that I need to be in Sunday school to study His Word every Sunday! Therefore, Janet and I are always in a Sunday school class for Bible Study on Sundays.

Another wonderful experience happened in my life during the year of 1988. God had me under conviction about my use of tobacco. He showed me that this habit was destroying my testimony. The Holy Spirit of God impressed on my heart that my family would never believe that I had changed because I continued to smoke. So in February of 1988, I finally asked God to take the desire for cigarettes from me. I would take it one day at a time. Glory to God because He took the habit from me that month!

In December of 1988, Janet and I sang in the Christmas cantata in Penelope Baptist Church and also celebrated our Christmas together with our families. We prepared for the next year in Gardner-Webb and asked God to use us for His glory.

After I received my class assignments for the new semester of January 1989, I began again to prepare to be the best servant by doing my best in my studies. Besides those classes in my major, I continued to take classes that I was required to take in the liberal arts field. Every class would be an experience that I was grateful for, especially the class in college math, which I did very well in although I had not had any math since 1961 when I graduated from New Hanover High School in Wilmington, North Carolina.

In the summer of 1989, the Lord opened the door for me to work in the seafood area of the Kroger Sav-On store in Hickory, North Carolina, which was also the store that Janet worked in. God would use me to talk to a lot of young people who were thinking about suicide to help them. In addition, I was able to testify and tell my story to many of those who worked with me when they would ask me why I was in the university.

I was also able to establish some good fellowship time with many of the evangelical pastors who would shop at the store, one in particular who needed to talk to another minister about some problems that he was having in his fellowship. After discussing what the Lord would do, we both were helped in being a leader and servant of His people. I was also able to build relationships with those pastors who were in Gardner-Webb religion classes with me. Many would invite me to come and tell my testimony and share God's Word with their congregations.

We watched the Spirit of God draw many people to the Father, and God would add to His church many folks during those opportunities.

CHAPTER 5

The new year of study at Gardner-Webb in the fall of 1989 began. It would include my second year of biblical Greek. I would continue to study psychology with various teachers. I also took classes in religious education with Dr. Alice Cullinan (deceased). Under Dr. Cullinan's teaching, I was able to study cross-cultural evangelism, which would help me in the future in doing world and local missions. Later in seminary, I would go on short trips to the nations as an international missionary for the International Mission Board of the Southern Baptist Convention; ministering in other cultures became a way that I could put to use what I had been taught in those classes.

In addition to that wealth of practical information on other cultures, Dr. Cullinan gave an assignment from one of her classes so that I had to study every part of ministry in the local Southern Baptist church. This I did in Penelope Baptist Church. I studied all areas of ministry, such as finances, Sunday school leaders and classes, deacon ministry, and other important areas of the local church. This experience would help prepare me for my calling as an evangelist and church planter for both the North American Mission Board and the International Mission Board of the Southern Baptist Convention. The classes also helped me to know to study and to learn other languages and cultures so that I could build relationships with the people that my Father would call me to do ministry with. I would also invest my life in these people when I was called to live with them in their country. Living with them would help me to learn about what they believed and trusted in when it came to religion and their hope for the future.

The Old and New Testament classes helped me to appreciate God's Word more. They were led by Dr. Logan Carson and Dr. Vann Murrell. These two men of God (both deceased) were great teachers and mentors who invested their lives in their students. Their classes gave me a greater hunger and desire for God's Word and to believe that it was true from the front to the back. They believed that the Word of God was all truth and that it was relevant for our lives, and I agreed with what they said because the Spirit of God gave me discernment that it was true. I began to notice as I was invited to preach in the different pulpits that many times God's message would be on the "Coming Day of the Lord" out of the Old Testament and "You Must Be Born Again" based on John 3, especially John 3:16 (NKJV) from the New Testament of the Word of God.

On many occasions, people would respond in obedience to what God had said to their heart either in the recommitment of their lives to Jesus Christ or in a personal commitment by faith to Jesus Christ as their Lord and Savior. I especially remembered preaching in one Southern Baptist church on the parable of the Pharisee and the Publican, using the passage of Scripture in Luke 18:9–14 (NKJV). Many folks there to worship that morning had left the home church over something small, but they were present because they were unhappy. They had left where God had put them to serve and to worship Him, and they were returning home. Besides the five who came forward to give their hearts to Jesus Christ for salvation as their Lord and Savior that morning, fifteen came in obedience to the Spirit of God back to where God wanted them to serve Him, together with the folks who were there. It was a great worship service that went over time, but God was pleased, and the people had their hearts clear with Him.

There were other Southern Baptist churches that I was called to to preach to their folks during the fall semester of 1989. As ministerial ministers of Gardner-Webb, we were sent to fill the pulpits that would be very fruitful for our Lord and His kingdom. Lives were changed by the glory of God and His grace through His Son Jesus Christ, and I continued to watch God grow me closer to the image of His Son for others to see. This was an awesome semester, but 1990 was to prove to me that every day serving Jesus would be greater than the day before.

The new year of 1990 would be awe inspiring with the experiences that Janet and I would have as we served a risen Lord! First, we were praying about what to do with the condo. In January, we had received a letter from Southeastern Baptist Theological Seminary in Wake Forest, North Carolina, that I had been accepted as a master of divinity student.

To fulfill my requirements for my degree in religious studies, Dr. Vann Murrell invited me to his office to tell me that I had been chosen by the religion department to be the preacher during chapel time for all students and teachers. This would be in February of 1990, during the student-led revival on campus. I was honored to be used by our Lord during this Tuesday morning time to draw all those present to Himself as I lifted Him up. I asked Dr. Logan Carson to sing before I preached, and God moved in that place of worship, changing hearts and lives.

Instead of preaching a sermon, the Spirit of God impressed on my heart to share where I was before I came to Christ, what happened when I came to Him by faith, and where I was now as His follower and servant. The Scripture passage I used was John 3:16, 36 (NKJV). The Spirit of God moved in the hearts of those present, and I was told that over fifty students gave their hearts and lives to Jesus Christ as their Lord and Savior! This time was anointed by our Heavenly Father, and many students would come to me during 1990 to talk about their relationship with Jesus Christ. For example, one student asked if he could talk to me after taking a biology exam.

As I was sitting on a bench outside in the courtyard, he walked up to me and said that he was lost, he just felt so lost in life, and asked me if I could help him. Within fifteen or twenty minutes, he was no longer lost but had his sins forgiven and believed that Jesus Christ was the Son of God, who had died for his sins! He prayed and asked Jesus to forgive him and save him, and Jesus became his personal Lord and Savior by faith in Him.

Another student had told her mother about me, and her mother gave her permission to ask for my help to drive her home to Newton, North Carolina. As we were riding in the Lord's car, I began to talk to her about her relationship with Jesus Christ and where she would spend eternity. I did not believe that she was listening to me, so I stopped talking to her. The Holy Spirit of God impressed on my heart and told me to ask her if she knew of any reason that she would not want to ask Jesus to forgive her and to save her. She told me that she had been confirmed in her Lutheran church but had no peace in her life. I pulled the car over onto the shoulder of the road, and I then led her to personal faith in Jesus Christ as her Lord and Savior. We rejoiced with her decision, and I had about twenty miles to disciple her. I told her that she needed to follow this decision for Christ with the believer's baptism.

Now this baptism was total immersion, as the Greek word meant, and if she asked her pastor to baptize her this way, he would do it. I also told her that she needed to be in a Bible-believing and Bible-teaching fellowship that taught that God's Word was all truth without error! This is and will be what I say and do to all the folks that Jesus uses me to draw unto Himself by faith.

Another great God experience that Janet and I had was concerning the condominium that we needed to sell before we left to attend seminary for three years. We were going to put it up for sale just before we left to attend seminary so we could stay where we were until then. But God had other plans for our lives that we would soon find out about.

Janet and I came home one day to find a note attached to our front door that said that a man wanted to buy our condo! This was in February of 1990, and Janet and I said to each other that if this was what our Lord's will was for the condo, then we would do it. We prayed over the price to ask for the place, believing that our Lord would lead us to where we would stay until December of 1990 when I would graduate from Gardner-Webb. Janet and I had a figure written down that we would ask for in order to sell the condo when we met with the gentleman and his lawyer. As we quoted the price to the man, he handed us a check with that amount already written down before he came to us. Wow! This experience that a Holy God allowed us to have was awesome, but we needed to be out of the condo in one month. Where we would go we did not know yet. We met with our pastor, Dr. Harvey Myers, to ask him if he would ask the deacons and the folks of

Penelope if we could stay in the basement apartment of the associate pastor's house across from the main church building. The folks of Penelope voted to let us stay in the basement apartment until we left for seminary and at no extra cost except to pay for the utilities! God sure is good to us! We would stay there until the last of August 1990 when we were forced to leave because of flood waters twice in two months' time.

Our Lord then allowed us to move just three blocks away for the same cost of paying the utilities until we moved to seminary. In March of 1990, we were asked by the pastor of Penelope, which was the mother church of the mission church, and the director of missions of Theron Rankin (there were over fifty Southern Baptist churches in this area of North Carolina) to help start a Baptist mission church in the Blackburn, North Carolina, area. The congregation was meeting in a basement of a home.

Soon, they bought a tract of land on Highway 10 between Probst's Crossroads and Blackburn Elementary School in Blackburn, North Carolina, on which to build a building for the folks of Blackburn Baptist Church. They purchased two trailers and set them in the form of a "T," and the Baptist men of Mountain View Baptist Church, led by Pastor Marion Powell (he would build the steeple that still stands as a reminder of the original building) and Penelope Baptist Church, including me, did all of the labor to build the building. We met to worship in this building soon, and we rejoiced and praised a Holy God for everything that He had done for His glory and kingdom. Blackburn Baptist Church asked me to preach their dedication message as they constituted as a new church in August of 1990.

I also was blessed that during this time, besides Janet playing the piano, I was also to begin to practice what I had learned at Fruitland and at Gardner-Webb in order to be a faithful servant and leader of God's church! This would be the foundation built on Jesus Christ that I would use in the future as an evangelist and church planter as an international missionary of the International Mission Board of the Southern Baptist Convention.

As I began my last semester in Gardner-Webb, I was allowed to do a chaplain internship in a local hospital in Hickory, North Carolina, called Catawba Valley Medical Center for my psychology class. I would go on Wednesday nights since many of the local pastors had services to do in their places of worship. The hospital gave me a place to sleep and all the meals that I could eat for free. I would start at seven o'clock at night and stay until seven o'clock in the morning when I would be relieved by the hospital chaplain. I visited every floor to let the nurses know who I was and that I would be on call during the night. I was soon called to the emergency room to meet with a family whose daughter had been in a bad accident. I met them and told them who I was and that I was there to help them in any way that I could, especially to pray with them and for them. The emergency room doctor soon came in to talk to the parents and told them that their daughter was okay and should have a full recovery! We prayed and thanked our God for intervening in the daughter's life and that she would recover from the accident. The family thanked me for being there with them and for being an encouragement to them.

After I visited every floor, the nurses would tell me which folks I could visit in order to pray for them and with them. One nurse on the oncology (cancer) floor told me on the first night there that two men were not expected to last through the night before slipping out into eternity. As I went to one room, the nurse attending to the man who was on a ventilator told me that his family was there in the waiting room, and they were concerned about his eternity because he did not know Jesus Christ personally. The nurse told me that all of the nurses attending to him were believers and followers of our Lord Jesus Christ, and they were concerned about his eternity and had been praying for him. I left and went to visit the next patient, who was dying. I stood in the room with the family and asked our God to surround that room with His perfect peace as one of His children was coming home to be with Him. The entire room was surrounded with God's perfect peace as His child took her last breath on this side of heaven and her spirit went to be with Him in heaven.

After I stepped out of the room, the mother and some of the first dying man's family came to me and asked me if I would please go see their son and brother because he was not a believer in Jesus Christ as His Lord and Savior. I went back to the room with the dying young man, who was only forty-two years old, and leaned over to talk into his ear. I told him that he knew that he was soon to slip out into eternity, and I begged him not to leave this world without Jesus as His Lord and Savior. I then whispered into his ear that if he would tell Jesus that he was a sinner and ask Jesus to forgive him of his sins and save him, then Jesus would save him. I then whispered into his ear that if he wanted to, he could say yes to this question. I whispered to him to squeeze my hand once for yes and then just trust Jesus to do what His Word said He would. He then squeezed my hand one time for yes to follow Jesus by faith, and the attending nurse immediately saw a change in his vitals. The nurse said that she knew that what I had said and prayed with the young man was real because she saw the change take place in the man's countenance. I walked out of the room and went down to meet and pray with other patients.

Soon, the nurse came to get me and tell me that the young man who was dying had woken up and was asking to see his family and me. In the time that I had come to be the chaplain for that night, the son of the man on his deathbed had been brought from the local prison to see his father. He was meeting with his grandmother, his uncles, and his aunts who had come from Indiana and were in the waiting room when his father was taken to the waiting room to meet with the family in a wheelchair by his nurse. The patient, who had just been on the ventilator two or more hours before, was talking to his family personally. I was told that he warned his son about living the life that had sent him to prison and he needed to change. He told his son that he had wasted his life, but Jesus had forgiven him of his sins and saved him. He told his son that he needed to ask Jesus to forgive him as a sinner and to come and live in his heart and life as his Lord and Savior. I left the family as they were hugging and praising Jesus for His grace to save their son and brother.

I went to visit some more patients on the oncology floor. Sometime later, after I was through praying with a patient and walked out of his room on the oncology floor, the mother and some sisters of the born-again miracle man who had been on the ventilator came to talk to me about baptizing their new brother in Christ. I told them that lack of baptism would not keep their brother and son out of heaven, because the thief on the cross beside Jesus was told by Jesus, "Assuredly, I say to you, today you will be with Me in Paradise" (Luke 23:43 NKJV). The thief on the cross did not come down off of the cross to be baptized, but he believed Jesus and what Jesus had told him. "However, if it means more for your brother and son to be baptized and you need that to believe that he is born again, then put him in a wheelchair, roll him in the shower, and run water over him!" This might not satisfy or be agreeable to many Christians, but it satisfied the family of the miracle man!

Another Wednesday night, as I was going room to room on the oncology floor, I went in to talk to a patient about his relationship with Jesus Christ and ask if he knew where he would spend eternity. He was good to everyone, he was not a bad person compared to others, and maybe God would allow him into heaven. I then told him that the only reason that God would accept him was that he had admitted to God that he was a sinner and needed forgiveness and to know that he would be in heaven with Jesus Christ and his family. I then shared with him what Jesus said in John 14:6 (NKJV): "Jesus said to him, 'I am the way, the truth, and the life. No one comes to the Father except through Me.'" I told him that Jesus does not just show us the way; He is the way! He does not simply reveal truth to us; He is the truth! And He does not simply give life to us; He is the life! I also told him how Jesus saved a false religious leader, which was me. I then asked him if he could know any reason why he would not ask Jesus into his heart and life to forgive him of his sins and to save him! He said, "I want to pray and ask Jesus to forgive me and to save me."

I led him in the sinner's prayer. After we gave thanks to Jesus for saving this man's soul, I then asked the son if he knew Jesus as his personal Lord and Savior, and he said yes! He also told me that they had been praying for his father for many years to be saved and he was going to tell his family and Christian family that his father was now a born-again follower of Jesus Christ!

When I was leaving the room, I told the father and son that I would be by to see them before I was to leave in the morning. When I returned to the room the next morning, it was empty! I stopped at the nurses' station and asked about the patient. They told me that he had left to go home to join his local Baptist church and to be baptized.

God had put it into my life to minister to people at the hospital and to thank God for those opportunities. Watching God change hearts and lives while allowing me to be a part of that was a joy and a blessing to me. Even ministering to those who had AIDS was a way God could show me that they needed His love and grace also. God was growing my spiritual life in order to show compassion and the love of Jesus to those patients and their families. This was an awesome experience for me to have so that I could be a better servant for my Lord to bring Him glory for my newly changed heart and life through faith in Jesus Christ.

Next came the graduation services from Gardner-Webb University in December of 1990 (I had to go back in May of 1991 in order to receive my bachelor of arts in religious studies diploma). Janet and I prepared to move to seminary housing in Wake Forest, North Carolina, to begin classes in January of 1991 in Southeastern Baptist Theological Seminary. We were finally able to have all of our furniture in one place as we settled into our new home and new chapter in our life. I must admit that I wanted to go to New Orleans Baptist Seminary to prepare for my life of service for our Lord instead of Southeastern Baptist Seminary because Southeastern was on probation. However, God called me to Southeastern not because of a diploma but because He was going to change that seminary to what it was to be for His glory and kingdom.

Janet was able to transfer to a store in the Raleigh, North Carolina, area with Kroger Sav-On. She was also able to keep our insurance in operation while I was a full-time student in Southeastern Baptist Seminary.

I had also applied for help from the Keysee Foundation Fund in Virginia, which was open to any Southern Baptist from the states of North Carolina and Virginia, and they provided all the finances for each semester that we needed other than what the cooperative program of the Southern Baptist Convention did. In addition, the Lord, through the cooperative program of giving among all of our cooperating Southern Baptist churches, would provide all the tuition for any Southern Baptist ministerial student attending any one of the six Southern Baptist seminaries. This giving, which I qualified for, took care of all my tuition for the three years that I studied in seminary. God sure provided all that we needed for all of my education at Southeastern.

The year 1991 would prove to be an exciting year of new experiences for Janet and me. God would begin to expand our borders and enlarge our wisdom and knowledge of His presence and power in and on our lives and ministries.

After we had moved into 38 McDowell Drive in Wake Forest, North Carolina, we returned to Hickory, North Carolina, for a week before going back to the condo in seminary. Much to our surprise, we had received new carpet and newly painted walls for the new beginning in our lives. God sure blessed us with the new beginning of our time at seminary.

We also began to visit local Southern Baptist churches in the seminary area in order to find a church home for us to serve in while we were attending seminary and living there. My watch stopped because of a dead battery. I took the watch to a jewelry shop in downtown Wake Forest to be fixed. I asked the owner where he and his family worshipped. He stated that he and his family were members of Hephzibah Baptist Church in Wendell, North Carolina. The pastor told me that they were in revival services, preaching the messages from God. After asking for directions to Hephzibah from Wake Forest, I told him that I had had the revival preacher as a teacher.

I went on a Wednesday night to worship and to hear the Word of God from a pastor I knew.

However, this was not the teacher that I knew preaching, but he was the man of God for the hour of preaching. The music was awesome, which led me to worship God before I heard the Word of God in the service. So Janet and I worshiped with the folk of Hephzibah that following Sunday, and the message from the pastor was on heaven (why you wanted to be there) and hell (why you did not want to be there). Seven people responded during the invitation time for salvation through faith in Jesus Christ! What a service! After a few more times of visiting, I was impressed by the prophet Isaiah's words (Isaiah 6:8–10 NKJV):

> Also, I heard the voice of the Lord, saying: "Whom shall I send, And who will go for Us?" then I said, "Here am I! Send me." And He said, "Go and tell this people: 'Keep on hearing, but do not understand, Keep on seeing, But do not perceive.' "Make the heart of this people dull, And their ears heavy. And shut their eyes; Lest they see with their eyes, and hear with their ears, and understand with their heart, and return and be healed."

It was here in Hephzibah Baptist Church that He wanted Janet and me to serve Him! This fellowship of believers grew in numbers every year that we were members because the heart of the pastor and members were evangelism, missions, and teaching the true Word of God. This would become our home church for over four years, and thanks to the leadership of the Holy Spirit of God on their lives, seventy-five people became members of that fellowship that came with us.

I was invited by a local pastor of a local Southern Baptist Church and a fellow student in seminary to go visiting. After we arrived at the church, the pastor introduced me to a man who worked with a lady who was one of Jehovah's Witnesses. He had been praying for her salvation for over thirteen years. He called the lady and asked her if we could visit with her that night, and she said yes. He had also told her that he was bringing me with him and explained I was a born-again former Jehovah's Witness. He asked her if that was all right with her, and she said yes. You must know and remember that I had become an apostate to the Watchtower Society, and folks were forbidden to talk with me under threat of being disfellowshipped. I do remember that it was the coldest night in February of 1991 as we traveled to Durham, North Carolina, to meet with the lady. We were not sure where her home was, but we went by her house with all of the outside lights on and with her standing at the front storm door looking for us. Soon she was standing on the front porch and waving her arm for us to come back to her house!

We went in and met the lady. We thanked her for allowing us to come. I then began to share my testimony of where I was before I met Christ. I had been a leader in the Watchtower Society since I was ten years old. I knew that there was sin in my life that I could hide from my people, but I could not hide it from Holy God. I also knew that one day I would have to stand in front of a Holy God and give an account of my sins and life, and I did not know how to have my sins forgiven. I then told her how Jesus Christ got me into a local church to hear the real gospel by saving my son, Ryan, and how he would invite me to come hear him and the youth choir of Winter Park Baptist Church in Wilmington, North Carolina. That Sunday night, I sat in my car frightened because I had been taught and believed that to go into any church not a Kingdom Hall was to walk into the devil's organization.

All these folk of Winter Park Baptist Church drove up, and as they left their cars to walk into the sanctuary, I went with them. I believed that God would not kill them to get to me. I told the lady that it was nothing I heard or anything I saw that that spoke to me that night but the fact that I was still alive when I left that made me seek God more. I then told her how the Holy Spirit of God led me to attend a Christmas Cantata and drama at Long Leaf Baptist Church in Wilmington, North Carolina, thanks to an invitation. I went in lost in my sins and needed forgiveness from Jesus. I was a broken man in spirit because I had watched everything dear to me leave me. Since I did not know Jesus Christ personally as my Lord and Savior, my wife had become my Lord. She had left me, as did my children, and God had broken me down to nothing so that the only way I could look was up to Him! I was looking at the large wooden cross above the baptistery, and I could actually see Jesus hanging on that cross! Jesus then spoke to my heart, saying that He gave Himself for me and my sins because He loved me that much!

When I realized what He had done for me, I began to weep from a broken heart. The folks of Long Leaf told me later that I was weeping so badly that one could have heard me from blocks away! The Holy Spirit had the heart and spirit of the lady ready to receive Jesus Christ as her Lord and Savior, and she knelt in prayer as I led her in the sinner's prayer. After she prayed, with tears in her eyes, she said that she finally had peace in her life as to where she would spend eternity. She then asked me if she could continue to go to the local Kingdom Hall since that was where a lot of her friends were. I told her to go because they needed to hear and to see the change in her life. However, I also warned her because of the Holy Spirit of God living in her heart and magnifying our Lord and Savior Jesus Christ, she would not agree with what she would hear! But until they made her stop coming, I told her to share her personal testimony of her personal experience with a Holy God. They could not deny or explain this experience away! We then told her that she needed to follow this decision with a believer's baptism and join a Bible-believing and Bible-teaching local church! Wow! Praise the Lord for a new born-again believer who had been lost as one of Jehovah's Witnesses, trying to earn her salvation through works and membership in the Watchtower Society. She was a born-again believer and follower of Jesus Christ. She would become the first of many Jehovah's Witnesses that I would be used of the Lord and the Holy Spirit of God to lead to saving faith in Jesus Christ.

My classes were great even with a divisive spirit in the different classrooms that tried to hinder the Holy Spirit of God. The classes that I was really blessed in most were the evangelism classes taught by Professor Dr. Delos Miles (deceased) and other professors. Dr. Phil Roberts was one of the evangelism and missions professors, and he was also the dean of students in the Baptist Seminary in Romania where he then lived. He took students on missions to Romania and I chose to go on my first mission trip to Romania in the summer of 1991. This would also be a class on international missions with books on Romania to read and a television show about the conditions for the people there and their terrible leader Ceaușescu. I began to pray about going to Romania, and the Lord impressed upon me the need to go. So I went with Pastor Rocky Gregory, with whom I had just gone through the schools of Fruitland and Gardner-Webb University. We were in Southeastern together, preparing to serve our Lord Jesus Christ. We got US passports and began to fill suitcases with all that Dr. Roberts had told us to take for travel.

In one of these suitcases, we would put items to give away to the people of Romania, who had very little. Since it was a class on international missions, we were also told by Dr. Roberts to keep a daily journal about the Spirit of God experiences that we would be witnesses of also. There were fifteen students, fourteen men and one woman, from Southeastern who signed up to take the international missions class and go with Dr. Roberts to Romania. We flew from Raleigh, North Carolina, to Atlanta, Georgia, on the large Boeing 747 with over four hundred people to Amsterdam, Netherlands, before continuing on to Budapest, Hungary. We prayed that we would be sitting beside folks who did not know Jesus Christ as their personal Lord and Savior.

When we arrived in Amsterdam, we were waiting on the next flight to begin. We found a restaurant and sat down to eat. We began to talk about what Jesus had done in the lives of those sitting next to us, and eight people became followers by faith in Jesus Christ as their Lord and Savior.

Already God had blessed our trip, and we had not arrived in Romania yet. We arrived in Budapest, Hungary, and were met by leaders from Switzerland with two vans plus a large trailer to carry our luggage. We then traveled by roads across the border of Hungary and Romania to where we would stay for a few days outside of Oradea, Romania. The country and places that we traveled through so far looked like our country did during the Depression and the years before! It was like stepping back to the early years of the nineteenth century, but this was because the people and country had been under terrible rule for over forty years.

The hotel that we arrived at just a few miles from Oradea was not what we expected, but we had to remember where we were. We were grateful to finally have a place to sleep and to take a bath before visiting the Baptist seminary in Oradea, Romania. While visiting the seminary and its classrooms, we would also meet the seminary students who would travel with us to translate for us during our time in Romania. We soon began to understand why we were told to bring towels, toilet paper, and bug spray for the mission trip. This hotel still had the old ball and chain toilet with toilet tissue that looked like our grocery bags back home! Their towels looked like our old throw rugs and were about the size of our face towels. The water we took a bath in was very dark so that we could not see the bottom of the tub, but it was nice to wash in. The food that we were served was great. The bread was as hard as could be but tasty with butter and jam on it! The coffee was very strong, and the cream that we used was different because it was from goat's milk. The sugar bowl had granulated sugar in it with a few protein friends that we left in the bowl. The food was great but different, and we would always pray the good missionary's prayer of "Lord, we will put it in, but will you keep it down?" We also knew that we did not want to offend anyone by refusing to eat or drink what had been provided for us.

For the next few days, we toured the Baptist seminary plus a few of the orphanages around Oradea that had been started by the local Baptists and Pentecostals. Here we also left some items from the United States for them to use and did worship services with them. On Sunday, the group went for worship in the Second Baptist church of Oradea, Romania, with some sharing testimonies, some singing praise songs, and Dr. Phil Roberts preaching the main sermon for all who were present. In the Romanian churches, the women must sit on one side and the men on the other side during the worship time.

This was an awesome worship time as we worshipped our Lord in different languages, but everyone knew that the Holy Spirit of God was the one speaking and leading the service for the glory of God. We knew in our hearts what He was saying!

The next day, half of the group went with Dr. Roberts south to Bucharest, Romania, to share with Baptist churches in that area before meeting with the rest of the folks in the city of Braila. It was here in Braila that we would do street preaching and a crusade in a soccer stadium for five nights, worship and preach in the local Baptist church, and help start new evangelical churches.

We would eat meals with the many churches and to do door to door evangelism in the communities around Braila. In addition to our group, Dr. Roberts had invited Dr. Robbie Maharge, a converted Hindu guru who would also bring over one hundred of his students from a Pentecostal Bible College in Switzerland to be our main evangelists. This group would camp in a campground near a beautiful lake, and they had brought everything to set up big tents for cooking and serving everyone along with small tents for the students, and we gave the students half of our bug spray to help keep the mosquitoes from biting them. The group had also brought guitars and other instruments to play while we sang hymns and songs on the streets and in the local churches. On the first day of missions in Braila, one half of the group went to the center of Braila to sing and to give testimonies as the Romanian students from the Baptist seminary translated for us to the crowd, and Dr. Robbie (who lived in Germany) preached and gave the invitation. We had one area set aside for the folks who had come during the invitation to be counseled and led to saving faith in Jesus Christ, and then we wrote their names down to be given to the local Baptist churches. We prayed with them and ministered to them. On that day, we saw God move in a mighty way, as over 150 people made a first-time profession of faith on the street! We were gathered in the plaza in front of the Romanian Orthodox Church, and the local folk would not come until the local priest began to ring the bells in the bell tower.

The people would come to see and to hear the gospel thanks to the ringing of the bells, and God would change their lives! Soon the man ringing the bells saw what he was doing, and he stopped. However, God sent a drunken man who danced while we were singing for Jesus, but the Lord used one or two of us to control him by putting a finger to our lips and saying no softly. The man was quiet until after the invitation for those who had raised their hands and wanted to come to Jesus Christ by faith came forward. For over six hours, God moved on the hearts of those who were there to come to faith for salvation through Jesus Christ as their Lord and Savior.

On another day, our group was in another park preaching, singing, and giving testimony to the grace of God through faith in Jesus as Lord and Savior on a hot and humid day. We were gathered where the shade was, and the local folk who were gathered were standing under the shade of the trees instead of coming close to where we were standing. All of a sudden, it began to rain everywhere. The local folk were standing, but not where we were standing. It was like the Spirit of God was telling them to go up close so they could hear the gospel message!

When decision time came, fifteen of these folks prayed for forgiveness of sins and for Jesus Christ to save them! One of these folks was one of our translators from the Baptist seminary who was not a born-again believer and follower of Jesus Christ. They made a personal decision to follow Jesus Christ as Lord and Savior. By the end of the week, there had been over fifteen hundred people who committed their lives by faith in Jesus Christ as their Lord and Savior. There were many new Baptist churches started during this time by our Lord. God added many folks to his local churches in Braila.

One day in Braila, the group from Southeastern along with some Baptist translators and a local Baptist pastor went to a large Romanian men's prison to hand out Romanian Bibles. We were allowed to visit some places that the men were housed in and the cafeteria that the men had their meals in. We were also able to share our faith with the guards and to give them Bibles. The large group of prisoners was led to a large room, which was also used as a gym, and the gospel of Jesus Christ was preached by Dr. Phil Roberts. In addition, we gave every man present a Romanian Bible, and for many men, this was the first Bible that they had seen and personally received in this communist-controlled country.

During the invitation time after Dr. Phil Roberts had preached God's Word, over thirty men committed their lives by faith to Jesus Christ as their personal Lord and Savior. This was a great day in the Lord for us and the men we visited. On another day, a large group, including those from Southeastern, many of the Pentecostal students, the converted Hindu evangelist Dr. Robbie, Dr. Phil Roberts, and the translators from the Baptist Seminary in Oradea, loaded a bus to go into a city near Russia but still in Romania. The bus with the group boarded a ferry to cross the Danube River. All of the passengers got off of the bus and could view the landscape along the Danube while standing near the railing. We traveled for over an hour by road to a city (I have misplaced the name of the city) where we would preach in the local Baptist church, and we did street preaching in the center of that city. Once again, we saw the Spirit of God move in the hearts and lives of the people. Well over thirty people committed their hearts and lives to saving faith in Jesus Christ.

We would also write down the names of those who had made any decision for our Lord and Savior Jesus Christ. We would then give them gospel literature and Romanian Bibles, pray with them, and ask them to also follow this decision with believer's baptism. Then we would give to them the name and address of the local Baptist church. We would also give the information that we had received from those folks to the pastor of the local Baptist church to do follow-up. This would also lead to new churches being started in areas that had no evangelical churches. Some of us traveled back to Bucharest, Romania, by train. The rest of the group from Southeastern traveled by van from Braila to Bucharest to stay one night in the Baptist seminary housing. We had left one van with the pastor of the Baptist church in Braila for them to use in ministry, so there was only one van for the group to ride in, and that was why some of us took the train to Bucharest.

We traveled from Bucharest by car and van to the airport in Budapest, Hungary, to stay one night there and then flew back to Amsterdam, Holland. We then spent a few days in an inn that was for visiting ministers who were traveling. This inn had been started by a Catholic monk and was cared for by four nuns as their ministries. We experienced our first hot showers in over a week, meals to bless us with fresh bread, and a time of seeing the sights in Amsterdam before boarding the plane for the flight back to Atlanta, Georgia, and then home to the Raleigh, North Carolina, airport. This had been an awesome, spirit-filled, spirit-led time of being on mission with God, and all of us were on a spiritual high! When Janet received me at the Raleigh airport for the ride back to our home in seminary housing, I was physically tired but on a spiritual high because of what I had witnessed a Holy God do! I told her that I was ready to pack my bags and go to minister to the nations! However, she said to me that God had not called her out of North Carolina or told her to fly on an airplane anywhere. Her decision would change over five years later as God would charge both of us to follow Him in faith and obedience by saying yes to His call to go to the nations.

Writing the paper for my class on international missions and doing cross-cultural evangelism would begin to plant the seed in my heart and life for God's call on my life after I had finished seminary. I can look back now and understand His promise given to me in Jeremiah 29:11 (NKJV) more clearly as I began to experience this new life in Jesus every day. Every time that I would read my daily journal from that trip concerning going on missions with God to Romania, I would believe that I was right back experiencing every day what I saw God do! What a joy it was and still is as I remember what took place while on mission with God in the world on that trip! The new semester in the fall of 1991 would allow me to have new teachers and mentors to pour into me what our God had poured into them. New opportunities to tell my story and to teach about Jehovah's Witnesses began to open up for me as an interfaith witness associate for the North American Mission Board of the Southern Baptist Convention. Also some of my fellow members in Hephzibah Baptist Church had family in the Watchtower Society, and they would ask me if those folks could talk to me. I said yes! Within one year, the Holy Spirit of God would lead three former Jehovah's witnesses to talk to me about where they would spend eternity. All three became born-again followers of our

Lord Jesus Christ! I would also tell them that like me, they were now born-again witnesses for Jesus Christ, and they needed to tell other folks about the peace they had.

Another ex-Witness was working with the ground crew of Southeastern seminary, and the Holy Spirit of God had him under deep conviction when we talked. I asked him if we could visit him on Saturday morning when he was off work, and he said yes. When we got to his house and knocked on his door, he opened it and, with a big, beautiful smile on his face, invited us into his home. He then told the brother in Christ that he worked with on campus and me that he had not slept all night. He told us that he got on his knees and asked Jesus to save him and forgive him of his sins, and Jesus did! He told us first before he told his family. I then asked him what country he and his family had come to America from, and he said Panama. I also asked him if their families were still in Panama, and he said yes. I then told him that he needed to go back home to let the families, who were Catholics, know and to let them see Jesus in his life. He and his family moved back to Panama two weeks later.

I enjoyed my classes with the professors that I chose in the classes that were in my master of divinity degree. Each one was used to help me to be the best servant of Jesus Christ that I could be.

The new semester would start in January of 1992, and I was excited as to what the Lord would teach me and the new experiences that Janet and I would have. We would continue to serve our Lord in Hephzibah Baptist Church, teaching Sunday school and doing ministries in a rest home in Knightdale, North Carolina. I had forgotten about a revival in a Baptist church in Dobson, North Carolina, in the fall of 1991, but the Lord reminded me so I could relate the experiences that God created in that fellowship. First, the revival committee contacted me to ask me to pray about coming for a weekend revival meeting starting on Saturday night and ending on Sunday night. I was asked to send them a picture of myself so they could put the picture and the personal invitation for the revival for the folks to come in the local newspaper. I wrote them a letter saying that I would be honored to come and the only picture of myself I had was a cutout photo of me from my Gardner-Webb annual, which I also sent. I was told after I got there, that when the letter was opened and the picture fell out, the folks saw a picture of a lady. They then turned it over, and there I was, which brought a sigh of relief to the committee. They also told me after I got there that the Lord had impressed on them to take me to a local photographer and have him take pictures of me for other folks to have, and the Lord provided over fifty wonderful pictures for me to have. The Lord moved in every service, and a total of eight new folks became born-again believers and followers of our Lord Jesus Christ!

One of these new believers had been prayed for by the local believers for many years, and he had come with his wife to the Sunday morning service. He had told his wife that if he heard that one must be born again to be in heaven that he would get up out of his seat and leave the church. Well, God's message that morning was "You Must Be Born Again" from the passage John 3:1–16 (NKJV). He did not leave, but he came forward under deep conviction to give his heart and life to the Lord Jesus Christ as his personal Lord and Savior during invitation time. He and his wife told me what he had said about leaving if the preaching was about one having to be born again to enter heaven! He said that he could not leave because the Spirit of God was speaking to his heart that he needed forgiveness of his sins and salvation from Jesus Christ!

Many of the young people would come after each service to talk to me about missions and service for our Lord Jesus Christ that they believed God was calling them to. I would help them to understand that you must start where you are in serving Him, and when He watches and sees your obedience to Him and His will for your lives, then He will give you something bigger and greater to do for His glory. In addition, a lot of families would come together for me to lead them in a prayer for their families as they wanted to serve and to seek God's will for their lives. We watched a Holy God change lives, heal marriages and lives, and add to His Kingdom those who would receive Jesus Christ as their Lord and Savior. This was also a great time for me to serve our Lord and for Him to use me for His glory!

When I began the spring semester of 1992, a lot of new professors had come from Criswell Bible College in Dallas, Texas. They were great conservative professors who believed that the Word of God was true and without error. This was to be an awesome year of a Holy God moving in the hearts and lives of both students and professors of Southeastern Baptist Seminary on that campus. God was turning His seminary back to one with a heart for obedience to God in evangelism, missions, and service to Him. In March of 1992, I was questioned by members of Penelope Baptist Church in view of ordaining me to the gospel ministry for my Heavenly Father God. On March 29, 1992, Dr. Dale Steele (deceased) presided over a worship service to set me aside for the gospel ministry by ordaining me. Reverend Garry Baker preached a charge to me and a charge to Penelope Baptist church as the ordination church sending me out to serve our Lord and Savior Jesus Christ wherever He would lead Janet and me. This was an awesome worship time but also a serious time of saying yes once again to answer God's call on our lives. I was asked to come preach revival in a Southern Baptist church near Iron Station, North Carolina, by their pastor, who had been a ministerial student with me in Gardner-Webb University. This would become one of the greatest experiences of the movement of the Holy Spirit of God in my life, as the Holy Spirit of God showed up in the services every time. This set of services went six days but had only been scheduled for four days originally. People were coming from miles away because the news of what our God was doing during the services was giving them the desire in their hearts.

God would heal people of their diseases, deliver them of their desires for cigarettes and alcohol, and save their souls. Sixteen people were drawn to saving faith in Jesus Christ as their Lord and Savior. In addition, we watched God put families who were going through divorce or separated to divorce back together. I can still remember this time of revival and renewal in the hearts of the people ten years later.

I would help two Jehovah's Witnesses to saving faith in Jesus Christ during the spring session in 1992 in Southeastern Baptist Seminary. The summer of 1992, I was to be a member of the praxis class on church planting for the North American Mission Board of the Southern Baptist Convention provided by Southeastern Seminary. The class was to teach students how to do church planting. I was to work with another Southeastern student doing church planting in Greensboro, North Carolina, answering the request made by the Piedmont Baptist Association of North Carolina. There were twenty-six students from Southeastern Seminary who signed up to go two by two into areas selected by the North American Mission Board. However, two weeks before my partner and I were to be in Greensboro to begin our church planting, he had to have surgery on his back and could not go with me.

Prior to me traveling to Greensboro, North Carolina by myself, eighty-eight students from the six Southern Baptist seminaries were invited to come to New Orleans Baptist Theological Seminary for a seminar on church planting. This seminar was led by the leader of the Church Planting Department for the North American Mission Board and would provide each student training in doing church training. I had the joy of sharing my story with all the people there and made the mistake of not calling my wife as I had promised her that I would do. I got busy, and I knew that I needed to call her, but I did not. The Lord made me stand and confess to those there what I did not do. I told them that sometimes I take my wife for granted, and the Lord reminded me that I should not. She had called me on Sunday morning before the group met for breakfast and the final time together crying! He reminded me that after my Lord, Janet was my first ministry. So from that time on, I told the Lord that Janet would be my first ministry as my wife and my helpmate.

While I was in Greensboro by myself, I helped the mother church that I was assigned to develop an outreach program through the arm of their Sunday school classes. While I was visiting folks with the pastor, I was used by my Lord to lead two people to saving faith in Jesus Christ as their Lord and Savior! However, I also found out that I was in the wrong place trying to do by myself what only the Holy Spirit and God could do, so I went back to Wake Forest. Soon, the new semester in the fall of 1992 began, and I was blessed with the teaching of some of the new professors and a very conservative person as God's man to lead Southeastern Baptist Theological Seminary into the future. Many more men of God were sent to help prepare the students there for their call in life to serve our God wherever He would send us. I was later to find out that I had twenty-six hours of classes on evangelism and missions, which would help me fulfill my Acts 1:8 (NKJV) call in my life. These were precious times in my life and in our ministries. I also received an invitation to come and preach revival in a Southern Baptist Church in Southport, North Carolina in October of 1992.

On my way to Southport on the Saturday before starting the revival services on that Sunday, I stopped at Long Leaf Baptist Church in Wilmington, which was my home church, to visit. The congregation was preparing for homecoming services on that Sunday that I would be in Southport. Here came a new brother in Christ, Victor Larkins (deceased), who had been one of my bosses in the paper mill I had worked in for over twenty-two years.

After I was saved by Jesus, I prayed for him to be saved through faith in Jesus Christ for over eight years. I would even call him on the telephone when the Holy Spirit of God would tell me to tell him why he needed Jesus as His Lord and Savior. He shared with me that morning how Jesus Christ had saved him on his bed at home. Wow! Vic and I were now brothers in Christ, and God has been using this man of God everywhere to tell his story about his Savior and Lord Jesus Christ ever since Jesus changed his heart and life! We had some awesome revival services in Southport with the Holy Spirit of God moving in the people's hearts and lives.

Many came to faith in Jesus Christ, many renewed their commitment to Jesus Christ because other things had become their Lord instead of Jesus, and many folk joined this fellowship of believers to serve their Lord there. Before I left to return to Wake Forest and my study time at Southeastern, one of the members of that fellowship gave Janet and me a cooler full of flounder already dressed to eat and fresh shrimp! Janet and I enjoyed this blessing from our Lord for many weeks. We were able to get away for some good rest and relaxing in Morehead City, North Carolina, during our fall break in October of 1992. I was able to show her where I lived for twelve years before my father Harry Lee Burns (deceased) was transferred to Wilmington, North Carolina, by Carolina Power and Light Company. We also visited Beaufort, North Carolina, and the North Carolina Museum located in the downtown area. It was there that I discovered that Otway Burns, a pirate off of the coast of North Carolina who changed his life, was in the Burns ancestry. He had two towns in North Carolina named after him with one being named Otway and the other Burnsville. He had a special section of the museum devoted to him, and it was noted that he was buried in the City of Beaufort's cemetery.

The spring of 1993 began my final year of preparation at Southeastern Seminary for serving my Lord with the rest of my life. I was able to preach in many local churches and to teach on the beliefs and practices of the Watchtower Society. I would do a comparison study between what Jehovah's Witnesses believe and practice and what born-again followers of Jesus Christ believe and practice. I also was able to watch and lead two former Jehovah's Witnesses to become born-again followers and believers in the Lord and Savior Jesus Christ. They sought me out thanks to family members, and I shared my story with them as the Holy Spirit of God drew them to saving faith in Jesus Christ.

The summer of 1993 allowed me to go with a group of pastors, professors of Southeastern Seminary, and other students on a mission to El Salvador, Salvador. We were able to preach on the street, in local churches, and in communities near El Salvador, where we would also show the Jesus film to the people. We witnessed over six hundred folks pray to receive Jesus Christ as their Lord and Savior while there in El Salvador. We also helped to start new evangelical Baptist churches. It was an awesome experience that all who went were able to have personally. Lives were changed, including those of the people who went on mission with our Holy God to El Salvador. God was also affirming in my heart and my life that I was to be a complete Acts 1:8 (NKJV) follower of Jesus Christ by obeying His call on my life to go to the nations of the world! When I returned to Wake Forest and to my wife, I told her that I believed with all of my heart that God had called me to go to the nations to tell my story and to lead people to saving faith in Jesus Christ as their Lord and Savior! I was also called to go and help start evangelical churches.

However, Janet said that God had not called her out of North Carolina or to fly in an airplane to any place. I knew that God would not call me to go to the nations without Janet! We were partners in marriage and in ministry, so I knew that the timing was not right yet. I also continued to be invited to many Southern Baptist churches to tell my story and to teach them about how to share the gospel of Jesus Christ with their families, their friends, and their communities for the glory of God.

I continued to teach a Sunday school class in Hephzibah Baptist Church that included the vice president of the Christian Motorcycle Association of North Carolina, John Fitts. John (deceased) came to me one day at Hephzibah and asked me if I would meet and talk to the son of the president of the Christian Motorcycle Association who had been disfellowshipped from the Watchtower Society in Atlanta, Georgia. I said yes and that I would meet him any place or at any time that we could agree on.

Soon, the father and son drove to a Southern Baptist Church near Goldsboro, North Carolina, to hear me preach and then to teach on the false Jehovah's Witness beliefs and the differences from the real gospel of Jesus Christ. After the services, the father, who was a new born-again former Jehovah's Witness, and the son asked if they could come to our house in seminary housing the next day to talk to me, and I said yes. After many hours of sharing the real gospel, the young man asked me if I believed in demons. I said yes because the evil one had many to represent him. I then asked him why he had asked me that question. He said, "Because I cannot look you in the eyes!"

I told him that our eyes are mirrors to our soul and spirit, and Jesus Christ was my Lord. Because he was a sinner, he could not look at a Holy God who lived in my heart! He left without committing his life by faith to Jesus Christ at that time. However, a few years later, he called me and told me that he had become a born-again follower of Jesus Christ and was saved in a service of First Baptist Church of Atlanta, Georgia, under Dr. Charles Stanley's preaching! He called me a few months later to tell me that he had said yes to God's call on his life to preach the whole counsel of God's Word! He was now in seminary preparing to serve our Lord Jesus Christ with the rest of his life. What a joy to my heart and spirit to hear and to see one I had prayed for say yes to God's grace through faith in Jesus Christ and then say yes to God's call on his life to be His servant wherever God would lead him. I still rejoice and give God praise and thanksgiving for saving this young man!

Soon, my last semester in Southeastern Seminary was to begin. I was excited to experience the next chapter in my life as we served a Holy God wherever He would lead us. As I was checking to make sure that I had taken all of the required classes for my master of divinity degree, I also discovered that I had taken twenty-six hours of classes in the evangelism and missions area while at Southeastern. This fact helped me to understand the area that my Lord Jesus Christ was preparing me to serve Him in as a real Acts 1:8 (NKJV) follower of Jesus. As I finished this chapter of my life and ministry, I was excited to enter into the next one.

CHAPTER 6

The years of 1994 and 1995 proved to be exciting in our lives and ministries as we waited on the Lord! Soon I received a call from the evangelism department with Dr. Delos Miles as the chairperson that I was to be the recipient of the John H. Clifford Evangelism Award for the year of 1993. I was presented this award at the opening convocation of Southeastern Baptist Seminary in the fall of 1994 by L. Rush Bush, the dean of the faculty. It was a humbling experience for me to be chosen to receive this award, and I give all the glory and honor to my Lord Jesus Christ for saving me!

In the spring of 1995, Janet and I knew that God was calling us to the western area of the state of North Carolina for me to be a chaplain in a prison in Morganton. So like Abraham and Sarah, we loaded a U-Haul trailer with all of our belongings and headed west. Janet also quit her job, and we were trusting the Lord would use her gifts and talents to serve Him wherever He would lead us. After we arrived at the apartment in Drexel, North Carolina, that we had rented, I went to the prison in Morganton to begin my ministry. The head of the human resources area of the prison told me that another man had been hired for the chaplain position. We then began to pray to our Lord, asking "Now where do we go?"

He impressed on our hearts to go back to Penelope Baptist Church in Hickory, North Carolina. Dr. Dale Steele and the associate pastor committee asked me to be an interim associate pastor and Janet to be the pianist for all the services.

After we said yes to our Lord for His call to serve Him in Penelope, He also provided the house of the associate pastor as a place to stay until He sent us on our next assignment. The Lord woke me up one night in the fall of 1995 to impress on me that He wanted to change the image of Penelope in the community around it. He revealed to me that He wanted the folks of Penelope to host a meal for free for the community. This meal was planned with chicken on the grill, pork barbecue, all the drinks and sweets, and bread and coleslaw provided by the people of Penelope Baptist Church for free. It was an awesome experience to be a part of. We watched our Lord minister to people through His children of Penelope.

The year 1996 came, and God was preparing to enlarge our borders to go to the nations with the gospel of Jesus Christ as International Mission Board missionaries of the Southern Baptist Convention. Janet had been reading a newspaper with an article about a local couple who had been appointed as International Mission Board International Service Corporation missionaries of the Southern Baptist Convention to Africa. She asked me if the Lord could use us overseas as missionaries, and I said that I didn't know. So I called the International Mission Board in the area of the International Service Corporation, and we were sent the full application process to fill out for them.

As we began to write, the phone rang, and I answered it. It was a call from the pastor search committee, and the brother in Christ told me that the committee had heard me preach six times in view of a call from God to come and pastor their Southern Baptist church. He said that the Spirit of God had told three people on the committee to leave us alone because He had something greater for us to do! This affirmed in our hearts that we were following the Spirit of God's direction and guidance for our lives to go to the nations wherever He would lead us! The committee also sent us a check that would help pay for all the areas of preparation that we needed to cover in order to go to the nations.

We were invited to go to a conference for the International Mission Board in September of 1996 to select, after praying over all of the assignments, the top three places to serve. We were appointed in October of 1996 to be the host and hostess of the Baptist Guest house in Rio de Janeiro, Brazil. After a time of thorough preparation at the International Mission Center in Rockville, Virginia, we departed on the flight from Charlotte, North Carolina, to Rio de Janeiro in January of 1997 on our first assignment as International Mission Board missionaries of the Southern Baptist Convention. Wow!

It was already hot at 104 degrees Fahrenheit at 10:00 a.m. in Rio, and then it got hot! When Janet and I arrived at the Baptist compound in Tijuca (an area of Rio de Janeiro), we moved into an apartment on the second floor. There were many International Mission Board Southern Baptist missionaries living in the four-story building, which also included a school for the missionary children to take classes with an international curriculum in English. Our responsibility included providing food for each meal time at a reasonable price, cleaning and preparing the apartments for people, receiving folks from the local Rio de Janeiro bus station or the airport who would stay in the apartment building, and moving people, especially missionaries, to their meetings in downtown Rio at the Brazilian Baptist mission office.

I drove a Volkswagen Cumby or van, which was the working vehicle in Brazil to move people and local translators for the volunteer teams from the US Southern Baptist Churches who came on mission with God to Rio to their places to stay and to do ministries. Learning to forget the watch in regard to time and to drive on one-way streets in this city of almost sixteen million people was a new experience for me. I also had to learn different routes to the bus station and airport because of the local high traffic times during the day. Until we learned the language, we would write out in Portuguese what we needed to say to the local stores, banks, and restaurants. Needless to say, however, we learned very quickly that we were the foreigners in this country, and then we got homesick for North Carolina and folk who spoke only English! This soon was settled by our Lord because He had called us to Rio de Janeiro to be on mission where He was working, and He would tell us when He was through with us in Brazil.

From that time on, we would never experience homesickness again in any future assignment by our Lord, because our home would be where God sent us. He would provide for our needs if we would trust Him by faith! Soon our assignment would change to work with the teams from the Tennessee Baptist Convention that would come on mission with God to Rio de Janeiro and surrounding areas for the glory of our Lord Jesus Christ. God also began to open up doors for doing ministries, as I was invited to preach in the local Brazilian Baptist Seminary and to teach the future Baptist pastors about what Jehovah's Witnesses believe so they could share our faith in Jesus Christ. I also began to teach a Bible class in English in the local Baptist church, which we had become members of, every Sunday. I was later invited to do a Bible conference and crusade in a Brazilian Baptist church near Rio. It would include preaching the gospel of Jesus Christ in a mission church of the local Baptist church that I was preaching in. In this area were five *macumba* (false African devil worship) temples, which I found out later had been praying against the Bible conference and crusade each night of the crusade. However, the evil one lost this battle, as the high priest and high priestess of a temple near the mission church who heard the gospel through the open windows came through the car garage into the church to become two born-again followers of our Lord Jesus Christ during the invitation time. They had to close this temple because the Holy Spirit of God moved into the area, changing lives for the glory of God. Also after the crusade was finished, fifteen came by faith during the invitation times to accept Jesus Christ as their personal Lord and Savior! Others also came forward to join the local church and made a personal choice to make a difference in their community for Jesus Christ and His kingdom. This was my first awesome experience of preaching the gospel in Brazil, and God blessed my heart and life to affirm our calling on mission with the Brazilian people.

Janet and I were enrolled in the local state university of Rio de Janeiro to learn Portuguese. Although we would use Brazilian Christians as translators, this would also help us to learn the language in order to know whether the translators were saying in Portuguese what we were saying in English. It is important that the translators speak in the first person what we are saying in English so we needed to know the language of the people. We also knew that we must trust the Holy Spirit of God to lead the services and speak through the translators the truth of Jesus Christ since He is the Word of God!

Soon we were going into the favelas (slum areas) around Rio de Janeiro with the other International Mission Board missionaries and the Southern Baptist volunteer teams from the United States doing evangelistic, medical, and other types of ministries in the name of Jesus Christ. Our first experience going into these slum areas located on the mountainous areas around Rio de Janeiro proved to be a blessing to Janet and me, as we saw our Lord change a young mother's life and to give her hope after her fourteen-old-daughter had run away from home. The young mother had also began to crochet a tablecloth with beautiful Brazilian flowers on it, and she gave us this tablecloth for introducing her to Jesus Christ as her Lord and Savior. We continued to visit her, and after much prayer, her daughter came home! We rejoiced with her over God's love to restore the relationship and to later become the daughter's Lord and Savior as Jesus became the Lord of the home.

Janet and I were learning that many in this area had no hope because they were so poor and living in areas that had no running water or electricity in the homes except what the people could steal from the streets. Janet and I were blessed to have these same experiences many times while in Rio as we were learning how to prepare for volunteer teams who would come there on mission. We were mentored by Reverend Benny Sprouse, Reverend Craig Steele, and other International Mission Board missionaries on assignment with the people of Brazil to help start new Baptist churches for the Brazilian Baptist Convention. Another time at our local Baptist church in Tijuca, Brazil, Dr. Bill Bright and his wife (Bill started the Campus Crusade for Christ ministries) came to preach. This was a time before he was to preach a crusade in First Baptist Church of Niteroi, Brazil. Dr. Darcy Ducelec, our Brazilian pastor and the president of the Brazilian Baptist Convention at the time, had invited Dr. Bright to come and to preach to our church folk.

Janet and I were blessed to personally meet both Dr. Bright and his wife and to have him sign a book that he had written for us. He is one of my heroes of the faith, and to meet him after meeting Dr. W. A. Criswell and the Texas evangelist Freddie Gage in one of our Sunday services in Hephzibah Baptist Church was a blessing! Each day, our Lord was revealing Himself to Janet and me during this time in many different ways, which brought joy to us and glory to Him.

Soon, I was also asked to come to the Baptist Seminary in Rio de Janeiro to share my testimony of my salvation from a false cult to a born-again relationship with a Holy God. I also taught these future men and women of God who were called into His service what the Jehovah's Witnesses were trusting in and about their gospel, which was different from the gospel of Jesus Christ that the Bible teaches. A person who is a sinner needs to by faith believe what the Bible says about Jesus Christ as the only way of salvation. When we know that we cannot save ourselves and only trust in Jesus Christ to forgive us and to save us, then we become children of a Holy God. Trusting in Jesus Christ as Savior and Lord is the greatest witnessing tool that a child of God has. The devil cannot deny that personal encounter with a Holy God, and neither can the Witnesses. So allow the Holy Spirit of God to lead you in what to say and allow Him to draw that one unto the Father through saving faith in Jesus Christ. This is what I tell everyone when I am asked how to share to Jehovah's Witnesses.

When I teach what they believe, I always use God's Holy Word to determine if they are a true religion or a false religion. In Deuteronomy 18:18–22 (NKJV), Jehovah God tells His people then and now if a prophet speaks in His name. Jehovah's Witnesses are taught that the Watchtower Society is the only prophet on earth that Jehovah God speaks through, and if that thing does not happen, God did not speak it! Many times, the Watchtower Society has said that events would happen that did not take place. They have also changed their teaching because they were wrong. I will also use what God's Word says in 2 Corinthians 11:3–4 (NKJV): if someone comes preaching a different Jesus and they do not believe that Jesus is Jehovah God of the Old Testament or the God man who is 100 percent God but also 100 percent man, then they are misled. The Watchtower Society teaches Jehovah's Witnesses to believe that Jesus is just the Son of God, which He is; however, He is the second person of the Godhead and the exact image of Jehovah God to mankind. The angels of heaven worship Him, and they only worship God the Father (Hebrews 1:1–6 NKJV). Since God the Father is Spirit and we cannot see Him, He came to earth by being born through a virgin woman, Mary, who was pregnant by the Holy Spirit of God.

In Colossians 1:15–18 (NKJV), written by the Apostle Paul through the guidance and direction of the Holy Spirit of God, the Bible tells us that Jesus is the revelation to mankind of the invisible Heavenly Father who is Spirit! "Firstborn" tells us that Jesus was none other than the preexistent Christ who is coequal with the Heavenly Father. "Firstborn" is the reference to His position in the Godhead and explains the quality of His relationship with the Father! Everything was created through Him and for Him as the head of the body and church of born-again believers and followers of Jesus Christ. Another verse of Holy Scripture that spoke to my heart as to who Jesus Christ is was Colossians 2:9 (NKJV), which reads, "For in Him (Jesus) dwells all the fullness of the Godhead bodily!" This passage affirms to me that Jesus is a deity and has all of the powers and attributes of God the Father. Continuing in 2 Corinthians 11:4 (NKJV), Paul tells us, "or if you receive a different spirit which you have not received" to not accept this fact.

To the Watchtower Society, the Holy Spirit of God is the Old Testament concept of God's Spirit, which is on you and not in you, as Jesus said in John 14:16–18 (NKJV). Jesus said that He would send another Helper who would abide with His children forever, and He (the Holy Spirit) dwells with you and will be in you. The Watchtower Society denies that the Holy Spirit of God is the third person of the Godhead; however He is a person and God the Spirit to all of mankind.

In Acts 5:3–4 (NKJV), Peter said, "Ananias, why has Satan filled your heart to lie to the Holy

Spirit and keep back part of the price of the land for yourself? While it remained was it not your own? And after it was sold, was it not in your own control? Why have you conceived this thing in your heart? You have not lied to men but to God." *He* is God the Spirit who lives in our hearts if we are believers and followers of the Lord Jesus Christ and helps us daily to follow God. He is there to help us in those times of moral, physical, and emotional weakness as He makes intercession on our behalf to the Father. Continuing in 2 Corinthians 11:4 (NKJV), Paul warns that if anyone presents to us a different gospel that we have not accepted, which is trust and belief in Jesus Christ as both Lord and Savior, not to listen. Instead of salvation through Jesus Christ as the only way, the truth, and the life as Jesus said in John 14:6 (NKJV), the Watchtower Society teaches that you must be one of Jehovah's Witnesses by baptism and do works to prove to Jehovah God that you are one of His witnesses.

Sin is a problem in the life of every person on earth, and Jesus is the only one who can forgive sin and save you. Before I became a believer and follower of Jesus Christ by faith in Him, I was always using one verse of Scripture when talking to people as one of Jehovah's Witnesses about the reality of death, which was Romans 6:23 (NKJV). I would quote the first part of that verse, and the devil hid the last part from my eyes and life. The verse reads, "For the wages of sin is death, but the gift of God is eternal life in Christ Jesus our Lord." Until the Holy Spirit of God revealed this verse and the whole Word of God to me after I was born again as a child of God, the evil one and men controlled me and my life! However, Jesus Christ has set me free because He is the way and the truth and the life, and he has saved me and forgiven me of all my sins of the past, of today, and of the future! You have just read what the Spirit of God has me teach and share about the beliefs and practices of a false religion around the world. I have had the joy and honor of being used by my Lord Jesus Christ to see many Jehovah's Witnesses have the Spirit of God remove the blinders from their eyes so they could know Jesus Christ personally as their Lord and Savior. Only Jesus Christ is the Lord of their lives instead of men and the evil one.

In the summer of 1997, Texas evangelist Sammy Tippitt (deceased) came to Rio de Janeiro to do a crusade in the Jacarepagua area, a suburb west of Rio de Janeiro. Also twenty-eight Southern Baptist pastors came with him from Texas and other states in the United States to do door-to-door evangelism and to preach in thirty different Brazilian Baptist churches in this area of Brazil. I was asked to help preach in one of the Baptist churches in Jacarepagua and to do door-to-door evangelism in the slum area of the Brazilian Baptist church.

Janet and I were able to visit many days with these people to watch seven folks become believers and followers of Jesus Christ. On the Sunday that I preached in the church, my translator, who was one of Jehovah's Witnesses and a student in the university in Rio and who had translated for me for two days in order to practice his English, made a profession of faith when I gave the invitation at the Sunday morning service. He had been listening to the Holy Spirit of God as I shared my testimony many times, and the Holy Spirit of God drew him to the Father when he knew that in his heart he was a sinner in need of forgiveness and salvation through faith in Jesus Christ as his Lord and Savior. There were many volunteer teams to come on mission with the Lord to the Rio de Janeiro area and surrounding areas during the year of 1997 with many decisions made to follow Jesus Christ with a faith-based commitment.

In the fall, Hickory Grove Baptist Church from Charlotte, North Carolina, came with a large team to do door-to-door ministries and nighttime crusades in a community just east of Rio de Janeiro. At the end of the week, many folks had become followers and believers of Jesus Christ as their Lord and Savior. God added over thirty folks to the local Baptist church, which included the high priestess of the local Spiritist and macumba temple! She no longer followed the evil one and his leadership, and after the local high priest told her that she had to recant the decision she had made to take Jesus Christ as her personal Lord and Savior, she said that she could not get Jesus Christ out of her heart because He was her Lord and lived in her heart.

Janet and I celebrated our first Christmas in Brazil in December of 1997 in worship services in Brazilian Baptist churches. The temperature was over a hundred degrees and very hot as we celebrated Christmas with our Brazilian Baptist brothers and sisters.

Our first year in Brazil had been awesome, and we were excited to see what our Lord would do in our lives in the new year of 1998. We had been witnesses to His awesome saving grace in the lives of folk who were poor and without hope. We were able to train translators in English, preach and teach in many venues, and learn how to prepare for the volunteer teams that we would use everywhere God would send us.

The year of 1998 would be an awesome year of experiences while on mission with our Lord in Brazil, North Carolina, and Romania. It was also a heartbreaking time for my wife, Janet, and me because of her experience with her heart.

The first great experience for me was to be invited to be an adult leader of our International Mission Board children's camp (for children thirteen to eighteen years of age) in Brazil, Uruguay, and Paraguay. The camp for our young people was held in a beautiful setting in the countryside of Brasilia. I was also able to share my conversion testimony and teach these great young believers and followers of our Lord Jesus Christ about what the Watchtower Society believes and teaches other folks in order for us to understand who or what they are trusting in.

I told them that their conversion experience with Jesus Christ was the most valuable way to share the love of Jesus Christ with anyone. Why? Because both the devil and those lost Jehovah's Witnesses or any unbeliever could not deny the saving grace of Jesus Christ in your life, which you have experienced. I also tell those that I teach to remember that only the Holy Spirit of God can convict people of their sin and draw them to the Heavenly Father. For those who are seeking God by faith, they can experience a personal encounter and a personal relationship with Jesus Christ as their Lord and Savior.

I was also able to cook American dishes for everyone there and to teach the Brazilian cooks of the camp how to prepare American dishes using Brazilian products.

Every morning, these folks would eat fourteen dozen eggs scrambled, fourteen pounds of bacon, and at least two hundred biscuits. We did have some Brazilian meals prepared by the Brazilian cooks, but I would fix spaghetti meals. I would cook and bake chicken and pork chops, American chili con carne and rice, and steak and baked potatoes with salad. The Missionary girls would make sweets, which included cakes, pies, cobblers, and other sweets that the boys and girls loved. We took them to Brasilia, which is the capital of Brazil, to eat at the Pizza Hut and shop in the large mall there. The young people also toured the president of Brazil's home and the place where the Senate of Brazil convened to make their political decisions for the country. We also took them to see various places of culture, including a large Roman Catholic Church, which was founded in the eighteenth century. This was an awesome experience that everyone who was present enjoyed.

I was also spiritually challenged by a personal study based on the gifts of God. This study was led by one of the ministers of Belleview Baptist Church of Memphis, Tennessee. In the first of March 1998, Janet was managing the Baptist Guest House of Rio de Janeiro while I was doing ministries with a college volunteer team from Mississippi and one of our International Mission Board missionaries based in Rio de Janeiro. We had just returned from our first vacation time in Cabo Frio, Brazil, and Janet had gotten very sick while we were there. We had three Southern Baptist ladies who were also nurses from America staying in one of the apartments of the guest house, and Janet was helping them do tourist sightseeing while they were there.

Janet got really sick. She was having grand mal seizures, which were stopping her heart from working. In three days, Janet's heart had stopped fourteen times both before and after she was taken to the hospital in Botafogo, Brazil, one of the communities of Rio de Janeiro. The doctors who were taking care of her at the hospital also had to use the paddles to revive her both in the operating room and her hospital room. I was asking our Heavenly Father not to take her to be with Him yet, and He impressed on my heart that she would be all right. The doctors put a temporary pacemaker in her heart because they discovered that the bottom half of her heart was not working, and the pacemaker along with a line going into the heart made the heart start working right. After the International Mission Board medical doctors gave the okay to use a Medtronic pacemaker. Surgery was done, and Janet was well enough to go back to her hospital room for healing!

I must also tell how our Heavenly Father took care of Janet during this time by having five Southern Baptist nurses from America take care of her before she was taken by ambulance to the hospital for treatment. He also had the number one heart surgeon from Johns Hopkins in America in the Botafogo hospital leading a conference on the heart. His daughter, who was his head nurse in John Hopkins, was with him, so she also led the team who did surgery on Janet! Some would say that this was a coincidence, but I know that our Heavenly Father divinely intervened in Janet's life to keep her on this side of heaven to continue to serve Him with a walking testimony of His Grace!

Within a few weeks, we were traveling back to Hickory, North Carolina, with an appointment in the Wake Forest Baptist Hospital in Winston-Salem on the first of April of 1998 with the heart doctors to try to discover why this had happened to Janet and her heart because she was so young! In the Baptist Hospital in Winston-Salem, the doctors did a three-hour heart operation and discovered what had happened to Janet's heart.

The doctors told Janet and me that a viral infection she had, along with her potassium level being down because of the extreme heat, and her eating so much made her heart stop. While she was in the Baptist hospital for almost a week, the doctors in the Bowman Gray School of Medicine of Wake Forest University along with their professors would study Janet because she was a textbook case that none of them had ever seen before! Finally, we knew how and why Janet's heart did what it did and were told by the heart doctor in Baptist Hospital what to expect with Janet's life from this time until she would go to be with the Lord or He would keep her in good health on this side of heaven.

Janet and I knew that our Lord had called us to go to the nations as His missionaries, but our heart doctor told us that we could not go into any country that had malaria and that there must not be extreme heat. He also told us that she would need to be in a country with good medical help, but he also gave us a heart transmitter to use to call the heart station in the Baptist hospital in Winston-Salem, North Carolina, if we needed to have her heart and the batteries in the pacemaker checked. He also sent all of the reports to the doctors of the Southern Baptist Convention International Mission Board, who would review them and give us the opportunity to serve again overseas. Before we contacted the International Mission Board to meet with them to determine where we would serve our Lord again as missionaries, the Lord gave us a car to use thanks to a Christian family. Two brothers and their father ran a salvage company that took wrecked cars and trucks and made them new so people could buy them. I was told that the car was the Lord's car, and when we went on our next assignment, we would give it back to him and he would give it away again. Also we were told that Dr. Mike Runion was the new pastor of Three Forks Baptist Church in Taylorsville, North Carolina, which had sent a volunteer team to Brazil on mission with God in 1997. We had hosted them in the Baptist Guest House in Rio de Janeiro. Janet and I went to visit Pastor Runion, and he showed us around the Baptist church, including showing us a fully furnished two-room apartment with a bathroom that was built into the conference building especially for visiting ministers or missionaries.

Janet and I had been praying for a place to stay, and our Lord told us that this was the place, so we asked Pastor Runion if we could be Three Forks resident international Southern Baptist missionaries, and he told us yes later that day after talking to the deacons. We moved in that following Monday and soon became members of Three Forks Baptist Church to serve our Lord there before He sent us overseas again. I had been praying that if the Lord could work it out, I would love to go to Romania again on mission before leaving on our next assignment to South

Korea on January 3, 1999, and God answered that prayer! Pastor Mike Runion asked me to go in November of 1998 with him and forty other Southern Baptist ministers and laypeople. I said yes, but I had no money to go with them. He then told me that the people of Three Forks would pay for the airline ticket, plus there would be a golf tournament I would play in. There would also be money taken up to give to me to go to Romania on mission with God.

As Pastor Mike and I were preparing to go to Romania, I was excited to return to the people of Romania to share my story and to introduce many to saving faith in our Lord Jesus Christ as I had in 1991 while I was in seminary. We were going the first two weeks of November of 1998, and the time there was to be cold but exciting as we were to become witnesses of the grace of God to many who would become followers of and believers in the Lord Jesus Christ by faith. We flew into Budapest, Hungary, and stayed one night in a local hotel before riding in a large European bus with the other folks who had come on mission with God to Romania.

After we arrived in Oradea, Romania, we stayed for a couple days to tour the local Baptist seminary and to worship in the Second Baptist Church of Oradea, Romania. It was an awesome worship time through music and the preached Word of God with the believers of Second Baptist Church in Oradea. In addition to worship time with the folks of Second Baptist Church, we also toured a couple of orphanages and did worship time with the workers and children, which was a blessing to all of us. We then prepared to divide our team into two groups to leave the next day for two areas of Romania to preach in the many churches and visit with those who were lost without Jesus Christ. Our trip would include prisons.

The team that I was assigned to went up into the mountain area of Bistrica, Romania, and other local churches to do ministries. As we got closer to Bistrica, we encountered snow, and it continued to snow while we were there. I was not prepared for snow because I had not taken winter clothes with me; however, God provided all that I needed through the people who were with me. People Three Forks Baptist Church in Taylorsville, North Carolina, also helped. One individual had given Pastor Mike Runion a large winter coat to give away to someone in Romania, and Pastor Mike gave it to me to use and to give away to a man while we were there. (I gave it to the pastor of the First Baptist Church in Bistrica when we were leaving)! Also one of the brethren with me gave me a cap to wear to keep the snow off of my head because I could not find one in our area of Romania that was large enough to fit my big head!

All of us were to experience many life-changing experiences and witness the changes in the lives of many folks. The Holy Spirit of God was present to draw them to a personal relationship with Jesus Christ as their Lord and Savior. The men would preach, and the ladies would do different skits based on God's Word. They would go along with the message that the Holy Spirit of God would preach through His servants in different Baptist churches, including mission churches of the mother churches in various areas around Bistrica. We also visited a large prison in our area where the gospel message of Jesus Christ was preached to a full men's prison with over ninety men making a first-time decision to follow Jesus Christ as their personal Lord and Savior. We were also able to give to every man there a personal copy of the Holy Bible in the Romanian language, which many had never had before because of the communist rule. This was an awesome experience for each of us present in the prison as we watched men hold the Word of God to their breast and to declare that this was the first Bible that they had ever seen and had been given! What a joy and a blessing to each of us to witness this experience and to realize how we as Americans can have many different copies of God's Word and yet read it very rarely. On the first Sunday in the Bistrica, Romania, area, I was taken to a Baptist church to the west, where I shared my testimony and preached on John 3:1–16 (NKJV) on "You Must Be Born Again to Enter Heaven!" Seven folks came by faith to Jesus Christ as their Lord and Savior!

I was then driven by car three hours away into the mountain area north of Bistrica to a mission church of the First Baptist Church of Bistrica, which was led in worship by one of the elders of First Baptist Bistrica. We had driven for over two hours in a snow shower and the last one hour on a dirt road with snow at least three feet high on the shoulders of the road to reach the little church building. When the service began, the church building was full of children, babies, parents, and older people from the villages near the church. Many of those present had walked over an hour in the snow to be present for the first international service with folks from Baptist churches in America. The sisters who were with me did their evangelistic skit, showing how Jesus can help you out of your sin and give you hope and a new life that will last forever when you ask Jesus Christ to forgive you of your sin and come and live in your heart and life as your personal Lord and Savior!

During the personal invitation time, the Holy Spirit came down into the service and over sixty children and adults committed their lives out loud as they prayed the sinner's prayer by faith to Jesus Christ to become their Lord and Savior! The next night, I went to preach in the First Baptist Church of Bistrica. I was later to discover that the pastor of First Baptist Church had been one of my translators when I was in Romania in 1991!

Before the service began, I was interviewed on a local Christian radio station behind the First Baptist Church of Bistrica. I was able to share my testimony and to answer many questions about the beliefs and teachings of the Watchtower Society of Jehovah's Witnesses. I also told the folks listening that the devil could not lie about their personal testimony and the Jehovah's Witnesses could not deny what a believer had experienced personally with a Holy God, so they should tell them what our Lord Jesus Christ had done for them. We must remember that we cannot save them, because only the Holy Spirit of God can convict folks of their sin and then draw them to the Father God for salvation. When I was leaving the radio studio, the brother in Christ who was the announcer asked me to sign my name on the door frame of the radio station for him to tell others that I had been on his program.

On another night, I preached in another Baptist Church near Bistrica where the Holy Spirit of God anointed the service and many people committed their lives by faith to Jesus Christ as their

Lord and Savior. Both the evangelism skit presented by the two sisters in Christ and the preached Word of God ministered to those there, and Jesus was lifted up high to draw people unto Himself.

On the last night of the crusades in the different Baptist churches of the Romanian Baptist Convention, I was taken to the Evangelical Baptist Church started by Romanian people to preach the gospel of Jesus Christ. The Romanian government had been studying the differences between the people there and the life they had been living. Instead of stealing and other bad habits, they were living and acting differently because of their relationship with Jesus Christ, who had changed their lives. The people of Three Forks Baptist Church in Taylorsville, North Carolina, had given to Pastor Mike Runion a love gift to give away in Romania, and when he found out this Baptist church needed firewood to continue to heat their building plus money to pay the lease on that building, they received the Lord's money. This took care of all of their needs for over a year!

Before I had left for Romania, Brother Vic Larkins (deceased) of Riegelwood, North Carolina, had given me a tie to give away in Romania. After I had preached in this Baptist church and during the invitation time, two older ladies came forward to pray the sinner's prayer to receive Jesus Christ as their Lord and Savior. After the service, the Romanian pastor asked me if I could give him my tie (the one that Vic Larkins had given to me) with the king's crowns on it to wear when he was to give to the two new believer's the King's Word on the following Sunday. I immediately took the tie off and gave it to the pastor. This had been a great time and experience for me. Our Lord had allowed me to be there and to worship with these precious folks. When our time was over in Romania, the two groups came back together to travel back by bus to Budapest, Hungary, and to tell what God had done in everyone's life while there on mission. God so moved that over four hundred folks had prayed to receive Jesus Christ as their Lord and Savior! We also left many Romanian Bibles with the people of Romania, and many believers in Romania were encouraged personally to meet brothers and sisters in Christ from America. All who went were blessed. Our Lord Jesus Christwas drawing many folks unto Himself by faith in Him as their Lord and Savior! The body of Christ in Romania was encouraged and loved on by the folks who went on mission there and whose lives were impacted by our Lord Jesus Christ also.

As 1998 was ending, Janet and I were preparing to go on a mission with God as International Mission Board Southern Baptist International Masters missionaries to an island off of the mainland of South Korea called Cheju. Our assignment was evangelists and student ministries on this island teaching English as a second language in the local university and doing English Bible studies both in our apartment and in the local Baptist and Presbyterian churches. We would leave Taylorsville on January 2, 1999, and arrive in Seoul, South Korea, on January 2, 1999, to have orientation with our Korean Baptist mission leaders for a period of time to adjust to the culture and our people group.

Before I write about my experiences in South Korea, our family had just buried our oldest daughter, Angela VanDyke Brown, after a three-year battle with kidney cancer. She was a bright light for her Lord Jesus Christ and a real Acts 1:8 (NKJV) follower and believer in Jesus Christ as her Lord and Savior. This was a celebration time for her family and friends because she was in the presence of Jesus Christ and was not in pain or suffering anymore! Praise the Lord! She believed the promises of God found in John 14:1–6 (NKLV), Romans 8:35–39 (NKJV), John 3:16, 36 (NKJV), and 1 John 5:11–13 (NKJV). Our lives will never be the same without her, but she was a real Proverbs 31:10–31 (NKJV) wife, mother, daughter, sister, granddaughter, and believer and follower of our Lord Jesus Christ! We all know where she is, and the only thing that separates us from her is time and space. However, unless you are a born-again follower and believer in Jesus Christ as your personal Lord and Savior, you will never see her again (John 3:1–16 (NKJV).

As Janet and I departed from the International Airport of Seoul, South Korea, on January 3, 1999, we noticed that it was very cold there. As we were taken to the Korean Baptist Mission of the International Mission Board of the Southern Baptist Convention in downtown Seoul, we were told that the chill factor that day was minus fifty-four degrees Fahrenheit and the large Hahn River that flowed through that city and country was frozen eighteen inches thick. Janet and I had never experienced winter that cold before. We were adjusting to the winter in South Korea, where we would join our Lord Jesus Christ for almost six years. We were pleased to say yes to His call on our lives to join Him where He was at work in South Korea. After many days of orientation to the culture of the folks of South Korea and the Asian world, including experiencing the wonderful food and the customs, we were on the Korean Air airplane flying to the island of Cheju to our assignment, which was with the students in the local university, tourists, college students, and church members. We would teach conversational English and do English Bible studies in our apartment with the students and those who wanted to learn English, which is the second language in South Korea and the Asian world. I would also teach English Bible studies in the Korean Baptist Church in Cheju City, South Korea, that we believed our Lord wanted us to join. I also was invited to teach an English Bible study in a local Presbyterian church, which was looking for a place to meet and study the Bible, so we invited the people to our apartment. God sure opened the door for us to have an English Bible study with students in our home. It would grow in numbers to include taxi drivers, professors, local pastors, and people who wanted to practice their English. Janet and I also had a Presbyterian Missionary family from Australia who were on the island of Cheju doing ministries for our Lord Jesus Christ join our group to help teach English and to add spiritual insight to our Bible studies.

As we attended the Good News Baptist Church in Cheju City, we were asked by Pastor Kim to share our testimonies and tell the folks why we were on the island of Cheju. Our translator Rajin Kim, who had just met us, spoke our words of testimony to God's grace in and on our lives in the Korean language to the congregation! As an answer to our prayers for God to place the people of South Korea on our hearts and minds to help us know that we were where He wanted us to be, the congregation stood up and sang a welcoming song to us in their heart language! Jehovah God spoke to our hearts, saying that we had asked Him to let us know that we were where He wanted us to be, and there it was! We both began to weep, as God had not taken the Brazilian folks out of our hearts but enlarged our hearts and put the South Koreans in!

Soon we were invited by the governor of Cheju Island to come to the local Far East Broadcasting Radio Station on the island of Cheju to talk to the station manager there about teaching the book of John in English on the air and teaching conversational English to the staff of the radio station. After arriving at the radio station to meet and talk with the station manager, we were both to be interviewed on the radio station to tell our stories of our life in Christ and how we got to South Korea. After Janet told her short testimony, including what had happened to her heart in Rio de Janeiro, Brazil, I was interviewed. I told how I had been a false religious leader for over thirty years as one of Jehovah's Witnesses and how I had hidden my sin, which I could not do enough to save myself or earn forgiveness for, from the people in the Watchtower Society, so I was lost. I then shared how Jesus Christ forgave me of my sins and saved me from an eternity separated from a Holy God in a place called hell when I had admitted that I was a sinner in need of forgiveness and salvation through faith and belief in Jesus Christ as my personal Lord and Savior.

The announcer then asked me to explain the differences between what the Watchtower Society believed and taught and the Gospel of Jesus Christ as Lord and Savior. After the time in the broadcast booth, the station manager showed Janet and me on the world map the people who would hear the broadcast in their heart language about eight or ten times a week for as long as our Lord Jesus Christ desired it to be broadcast. The countries who would hear this broadcast were China, Russia, North and South Korea, and seven islands in the Pacific, including Guam, Japan, and the Philippines. Janet and I were blessed to know that our Lord would call us to a little island called Cheju to share our faith with over one billion people while we were there. This was an awesome faith experience for the both of us and allowed us to grow our faith in Jesus Christ.

Two weeks later, the leader of the Korean Baptist chaplains in the army of South Korea called me and asked me if I would help sixty-seven Evangelical pastors and missionaries baptize almost five thousand new believers and followers of our Lord Jesus Christ in the army of South Korea. We helped baptize 4,254 new believers that day as they committed themselves in obedience to follow Jesus Christ with their lives. Dr. Billy Kim, who was president of the Baptist World Alliance and pastor of the Global Mission Evangelical Baptist Church in Seoul, South Korea, at the time, preached the sermon, and many of us missionaries and pastors prayed that Jesus would call out over one thousand of these young men to be His missionaries around the world. What an awesome faith experience this was to all who were used by our Lord Jesus Christ to help these new believers to follow His example with believer's baptism!

Janet and I were invited to teach conversational English in the local university, which would open up many doors of ministries for us on the island of Cheju. Many of these students would join our English Bible study in our apartment to practice hearing and speaking English. Also many of these students had been lifetime Buddhism followers because their families were practicing

Buddhist. Soon many of these students would become born-again followers of Jesus Christ as their Lord and Savior, and Jesus would use them to help their parents to come to Jesus Christ by faith in Him as their Lord and Savior. Years later, as we asked Jehovah God to show us what fruit He had done for His Son and kingdom through that Bible study, He revealed to us that four families and three single South Korean Baptist families were now missionaries in seven countries, sharing the love of Jesus Christ with those different folks and watching Jesus Christ change their hearts and lives through faith in Him as their Lord and Savior. What a joy it was to mentor these folks and to help them to follow the will of God for their lives.

In the summer of 1999, we, along with other International Mission Board Southern Baptist missionaries in South Korea, hosted Baptist Student Union students from the University of Georgia and the Georgia Institute of Technology, who had come to do student ministries on the university and college campuses on the island of Cheju. They were used by our Lord Jesus Christ to make an impact in the lives of those South Korean students, with many becoming believers and followers of Jesus Christ by faith. This also allowed those of us International Mission Board missionaries on Cheju to start Bible studies in English and to be asked by the local Baptist churches to teach an English Bible study in the six Korean Baptist churches. Janet and I were asked by the Southern Baptist missionaries serving in Seoul, South Korea, to help them do an English camp for South Korean children ages eight to twelve years old in Seoul. Janet would be the mother and grandmother figure to help the children to adjust to being away from their parents by loving on them and helping them talk to their parents on the telephone to calm their fears. I was the chaplain, the dorm parent over boys eight to twelve years old, and the teacher to do the Bible story time each day with the children.

By the time the week came to an end, forty-one children prayed out loud the sinner's prayer to receive Jesus Christ as their Lord and Savior and to follow Him as a born-again believer for the rest of their lives. This was an awesome commitment time, and all who were present witnessed the power of the Holy Spirit of God to draw people to the Lord Jesus Christ as their Lord and Savior. Janet and I were blessed by our Lord during the time of the English camp with the personal experiences we had with the children.

In the fall of 1999, Janet and I had the joy and honor to have a commitment service during our English Bible study time in the Lord's home for two of the young Korean college students who were going on international missions in two countries with the On Mission team in South Asia for one year. These students were used in a mighty way as real Acts 1:8 (NKJV) servants of our Lord Jesus Christ as personal witnesses to the life-changing presence of our Lord Jesus Christ. Our home Bible study grew in numbers during this time, and many students would go to the mainland universities and become great Acts 1:8 (NKJV) followers on the different campuses for Jesus Christ. Our English Bible study in the local Baptist church grew in numbers and in the knowledge of the Word of God as we studied the Word of God.

On the night that I taught on baptism and why we need to follow the example of our Lord Jesus Christ with believer's baptism, I found that eight followers of Jesus Christ had never been baptized. In two weeks, Pastor Kim had a baptism service, and these eight evangelical Korean Baptist students were baptized in obedience to our Lord Jesus Christ. Thanks to our God for His grace and love as we obediently follow Jesus Christ in believer's Baptism like these Korean Baptist students did. I also noticed that many of Pastor Kim's sermons on Sunday mornings were taken from the passages that we had studied with the Korean students on the Wednesday night Bible Studies. This was a blessing to me, as I would hear what God had to say to those people who were in Sunday morning worship time from His Word, which He had allowed me to teach to the students on Wednesday nights.

As the year 1999 was drawing to an end, Janet and I were aware of the many folks God had brought into our lives and allowed us to minister to and to mentor in the faith of Jesus Christ. The year had been an awesome time of developing spiritual and physical relationships that would continue down through time in our lives.

As the year 2000 began, Janet and I were growing in our own personal walk of faith as we had studied *Experiencing God* by Henry Blackaby together. We would also continue to study this book of wisdom and use it in our ministries in many countries to tell people how this book would help everyone to discover God's personal plan for their lives.

I met with a Christian businessman with twenty-eight employees in the early spring of 2000. I agreed to teach conversational English since English was the second language in the Asian world. After much prayer to seek God's help in this area, I had my daughters, Angela Brown and Tracy Chapman, mail us the Wednesday grocery ads from the local Hickory and Taylorsville newspapers. I also used the English inserts from the Seoul, South Korea, newspaper that we received for the students to practice with at home as they learned English. Most important, I was led by the Holy Spirit to use the evangelistic Billy Graham tract *Steps to Peace with God*, which has the Korean and English languages side by side for them to study and to practice reading English. At the end of the twelve week English class, I asked the group of twenty-eight to bring the tract to class for us to read and to answer the question at the end of the tract.

Twenty-three of these folks prayed out loud the sinner's prayer to believe and to trust Jesus Christ as their personal Lord and Savior! I then understood what the Lord had said to me when I told Him that I did not know how to teach these folks, and He told my heart that He would teach me what to do and to speak through me as He had done with Moses, Joshua, and Jeremiah. He must receive all of the glory for the decisions made by the students to follow Jesus Christ as their Lord and Savior.

As the summer of 2000 was soon to begin on Cheju Island, the six Korean Baptist churches, along with our International Mission Board Southern Baptist missionaries and Christians from many of the Korean Baptist churches on the mainland of South Korea, joined together for an evangelistic crusade on the island of Cheju. The major theme was based on John 21:11 (NKJV): "Simon Peter went up and dragged the net to land, full of large fish, one hundred and fifty-three;

and although there were so many, the net was not broken" (NKJV). I had never seen this verse used as an evangelistic theme before, but after the time period of the crusade, there were 156 new believers and followers of Jesus Christ. I have never forgotten how our Lord used this verse to see people come to Him by faith!

In July of 2000, Janet and I were asked by our Korean Baptist Mission International Mission Board leaders to prepare to lead the 2002 World Cup Ministries for them and the Korean Baptist Convention. We were asked to move to the city of Busan, South Korea, and to prepare for both the World Cup of 2002, held in both Japan and South Korea, and a large Asian Games (a smaller version of the Olympics with forty-four countries participating in the games) in the city of Busan, South Korea.

After a few months at home in Taylorsville, Janet and I arrived in Busan to our apartment on the eastern side of the city. I had also been asked by our International Mission Board leaders to join with a group of Southern Baptist pastors and laypeople from the Georgia Baptist Convention and many Southern Baptist churches in Georgia to do evangelistic crusades in the country of South Korea. I was able to join with these folks on five crusades over the next three years to witness over fifteen thousand South Koreans become believers and followers of Jesus Christ.

Many of these folks had been lifetime Buddhists and were over fifty years old. Using the evangelistic tract *Steps to Peace with God* in English and Korean, my translator and I in the last crusade presented the gospel of Jesus Christ forty-six times and over fifty people prayed to receive Jesus Christ as their Lord and Savior! More than ten of them were over the age of sixty, including five ladies over the age of eighty. These people had never heard the gospel of Jesus Christ! These were awesome times of witnessing the grace of our Lord and how the Holy Spirit of God is the leader in a witnessing encounters to draw people to faith in Jesus Christ. I want everyone to know that the Korean Baptist congregations had bathed each crusade with over one year of prayers for those folks in their areas of South Korea.

At the end of each crusade, there would be a time of reporting and rejoicing at a hotel in Seoul before the group from Georgia would leave for the United States. Every believer—pastors, laypeople, the leadership of the Georgia Baptist Convention from Georgia who had been on mission with our Lord at each crusade, and our International Mission Board Southern Baptist missionaries—would hear what God had done in the lives of the new believers and followers of Jesus Christ and would give to Him all of the glory.

When I returned to Busan to prepare for our assignment for both large sporting events, Janet had met two lady independent Bible Baptist missionaries and had been invited to join a Bible study fellowship study in English at a local Presbyterian church. This would open up many doors of ministries in local churches with children and women for her, which would allow the Lord to expand her borders for the joy of the Lord Jesus Christ and His kingdom. In this way, the Lord would also open up doors for me to preach in English in Baptist and Presbyterian churches around

Busan. I would witness many come to know Jesus Christ as their Lord and Savior as I preached from John 3:1–16 (NKJV), explaining why there are no grandchildren in heaven but one must be born again by the Spirit of God to become one of God's children and be in heaven with Jesus.

The door would also open up for me to teach an English Bible study with college and career Korean students in the International Presbyterian congregation in the church we would also worship in on Haeundae Beach. The Presbyterian pastor would also ask me to preach His Word from his English Bible for those present. We saw the Holy Spirit of God move in a mighty way many times as He drew those without faith in Jesus Christ to saving faith. I was also able through the Spirit of God's leadership to say "thus said the Lord" from His Holy Word to help everyone know Him more fully as their Lord and how to live for Him daily.

In 2001, Janet and I were allowed to visit many conferences of the Major Sports Events Partners in Grapevine, Texas, and Indianapolis, Indiana. This group, which includes the International Mission Board of the Southern Baptist Convention, is an evangelical group and Bible society that plans and prepares for World Cup and the Olympic events to do mass evangelism. This time would allow Janet and me to meet those whose resources we could use to prepare evangelical guides with the gospel of Jesus Christ presented in seven languages to help us to prepare for the two major sporting events that would occur in South Korea. There were many guides printed in four major languages thanks to the gifts given through the Lottie Moon offering by the Southern Baptist folks of over forty thousand churches in the United States. They were personally handed to every spectator who came to the ten different soccer stadiums in South Korea. The spectators would also receive the Jesus film on CD and DVD in different languages, another booklet with the directions to the stadiums from the subways and local buses, and an evangelical handkerchief with Bible verses on it, which an evangelical high school class helped produce. They received all of the gifts together.

In addition, I was allowed to visit along with five of our International Mission Board Southern Baptist missionaries from South Korea and the Korean American Southern Baptist Convention people from over seven hundred Korean American Southern Baptist Churches representative there. All of us were introduced to the people using a Korean translator, and we were able to talk about our ministries in South Korea. When I spoke, I was able to ask for help from those believers who spoke fluent English and Korean. I asked them to come on mission with God to help Janet, me, and the local missionaries and evangelicals of the Great Commission Partners to evangelize for Jesus Christ during the World Cup and Asian Games time period. I was able to tell them that if they came to Busan, South Korea, during the Asian Games, they would be hosted by the Asian Games leaders. All who came would be received at the Busan International Airport and clothed and housed in the Olympic Village, which would have over eighteen thousand athletics hosted by the Asian Games leaders. We would also be allowed to do worship services in an area where we could give away Bibles in four languages and the Jesus film in five languages and visit with those who came. In addition to this need, we invited them to come during the World Cup time to help, along with the other

Southern Baptist volunteers who would come on mission to South Korea. Janet and I also had requested and prayed that our International Mission Board and Southern Baptist churches would send people on mission with God to South Korea in 2002. Therefore, the rest of 2001 was preparing for the World Cup and Asian Games until I had to come to Hickory because of a medical emergency.

We flew home two days prior to September 11, 2001, and after a time of rest and having good health, according to my local doctor, Janet and I returned to Busan on the first of December 2001. We then began to prepare to receive Frank and Jennie Hong, two International Mission Board missionaries of the Southern Baptist Convention to help us to prepare for the World Cup of 2002 and the Asian Games held in Busan, South Korea, during the months of September and October. Frank Hong (now deceased) and I would visit six of the ten cities hosting the World Cup in South Korea and mobilize the Great Commission Evangelicals to do evangelism at the four stadiums that Frank and I could not be at. Since the games were being played at those stadiums in the different cities on the same days, Frank and I were to be in Taejon and Cheju City, South Korea with volunteer teams to do evangelism and provide water, drinks, and other needs for those who were at the games. I hosted a volunteer team from a Southern Baptist church in California along with local evangelical Korean Christians in Taejon, and we were allowed to pray over every seat in the stadium. In addition, we were allowed to put up our booths in front of a local Korean Baptist church to give out water and drinks, do face painting with those fans walking to the stadium, give out Jesus DVDs and other evangelical materials, and feed those who were hungry inside the Baptist church. We witnessed over one hundred folks commit their lives to saving faith in Jesus Christ. We also had a group of Navigators from Campus Crusade for Christ do a silent skit on Jesus Christ's birth, death, and resurrection for the folks who would stop, watch, and listen to the message of the real gospel of Jesus Christ. Our team was also able to preach in six different churches and one Presbyterian church in Taejon, South Korea. There were over thirty folks prayed to receive Jesus Christ as their Lord and Savior during the commitment time of the services. In addition, we were also able to do our own World Cup at the Christian school. We were given their dorms, cafeteria, and kitchen to prepare our meals for the team. Each day started with a devotion time and testimony by different people, and we ate well and were allowed to cook and make meals to take with us to the Baptist church near the soccer stadium. We invited seven universities in the Taejon, South Korea, area to play in the tournament, and we also formed a team from our International Mission Board missionaries and some of the folks from the volunteer team in California.

On the second round of the first day of the tournament, our tall mission pastor and former International Mission Board missionary to Africa from California volunteered to be the goalie for the Vietnamese team. Because of this act, after the tournament, he was asked to come to the home of the coach of the Vietnamese team to join the group of over twenty family members for a meal. He gave a word of testimony for Jesus Christ and told why he had come to South Korea. When he gave an invitation for the folks to pray for forgiveness and salvation, twenty-five people prayed the sinner's prayer to receive Jesus Christ as their Lord and Savior.

Frank was in the southern part of Cheju Island, where the World Cup stadium was built, to mobilize the Great Commission people and the local Baptist churches to do ministries during the games on the Island of Cheju. Many folks came to saving faith in Jesus Christ. Medical attention was given to folks under the tent where Christian doctors and nurses were there to do this ministry. The volunteer team gave out Jesus DVDs, guides for the games, gospel tracts, gospel handkerchiefs, and other evangelical materials as well as food. These were wonderful days to bring glory to God and to lift up Jesus Christ so that the Holy Spirit of God could draw folks to Jesus as Lord and Savior. After the World Cup games of 2002 were over, Frank and I began to prepare for the Asian games held in Busan during the months of September and October of 2002.

We were allowed to provide fifty Baptist folks from our Korean-American Baptist Convention in the United States, along with our local International Mission Board Southern Baptist Convention missionaries in the village where the athletes of the forty-four nations would be staying. Many from these nations were not evangelical Christians, so we were allowed to have a place for worship and counseling and to give away evangelical materials, including Bibles. Since Janet and I had resigned to return to Hickory to take care of her mother, who had broken two hips during the year of 2002, Frank Hong led the ministries during the Asian Games.

After the games were complete, eighty-eight athletes became followers and believers of Jesus Christ with many of these converted Muslims who had also received English Bibles to read. The year 2002 had become one of the greatest years of our lives and ministries. We praise our Lord Jesus Christ for using us for His glory and honor.

Over six hundred thousand evangelical gospel guides in five languages had been given away. Over two thousand Jesus Christ DVDs and eight hundred gospel handkerchiefs had also been given away, and over twenty-five thousand copies of God's Holy Bible in five languages were given to folks.

Many of us have seen and witnessed a mighty move of God's Spirit changing people's lives in many languages during this year of 2002.

As the year of 2003 began, Janet and I were soon to begin a new chapter in our lives as caregivers of Mrs. Edith Britain Rhoney, Janet's mother. I would be her preacher, her personal cook, and her chauffeur for over a year. In addition, Janet would become the assistant activities director of the assisted living home that her mother lived in, and I would become a volunteer chaplain for a rehabilitation center. Also, we would be able to share our stories in many Southern Baptist churches, telling others about what our Heavenly Father was doing in the lives of folks around the world. We would be Acts 1:8 (NKJV) witnesses to our Lord, calling many folks to the nations with the message of the gospel of Jesus Christ.

After Mrs. Rhoney went to be with her Lord Jesus Christ on His birthday in December of 2003, Janet and I heard the Spirit of God impress on our hearts to once again go to the nations with the message of Jesus Christ to see people become believers and to help start evangelistic churches.

CHAPTER 7

After we went to meet with the leaders of our International Mission Board of the Southern Baptist Convention, we said yes to God's call on our lives to Curitiba, Brazil, as evangelists and church planters in July of 2004. So we began a new chapter in our lives to help start an International Baptist Church in Curitiba in conjunction with Bacacheri Baptist Church, as the mother church for the Brazilian Baptist Convention of Curitiba, Brazil. We began by teaching a Bible study using the book *Experiencing God* in English. This Bible study grew to over thirty folks in four months.

Prior to this time, Janet and I were in Portuguese language classes in our International Mission Board language school in Campinas, Brazil. We arrived in Curitiba, Brazil, in late October of 2004 after our graduation time to begin a new chapter in our lives as evangelists and church planters, helping to start an international Baptist church in Curitiba for the over one million internationals whose common language was English. This would become the mother church to many churches in the different languages of the local people living and working in Curitiba, Brazil.

Once we had arrived in Curitiba, we went to the local Brazilian police department to notify the police that we were now living there and to fill out immigration forms for our visas to live and work in Brazil. After developing a brochure about the International Community Baptist Church meeting in a building provided by the mother church, Bacacheri Baptist Church, and their pastor, Doctor L. Silvado and congregation, Janet and I were able to provide information for those immigrants who would register with the local police department. We were also able to give English Bibles to those police working in the immigration department plus other English Christian reading materials in the waiting rooms for the people to read. This avenue helped bring many people to our services when we began in March of 2005.

We were also able to place our international community church brochures in many of the local hotels and businesses, which would bring a lot of seekers of Brazilians who wanted to practice hearing and speaking English as well as internationals who spoke English to our weekly services. I also took the English and Portuguese versions of the Evangelical tract *Steps to Peace with God* and had one tract made with these languages side by side to use with our volunteer teams who would come from our Southern Baptist churches in America to be on mission with our Lord. These groups would also work with the local Brazilian Baptist Convention churches to help start new evangelical Baptist churches in areas around Curitiba that had no evangelical churches in their areas.

Together with a team of Brazilian folks from First Baptist Church of Curitiba, we would place a circus tent near a medical bus and bring a team from America to do mass evangelism, children's ministries, door-to-door visitation, ministries in the local schools, and crusades at night. We would also do prayer walks with the Brazilian Baptists from those Baptist churches that would become the mother church and do the follow-up visits in the areas where we helped start a new church. Our Lord would use these methods to help start ten new Brazilian Baptist churches in and around Curitiba, where no Evangelical churches had been before, and services would be conducted in the language of the people. In addition, we had Southern Baptist construction teams come from First Baptist in Springdale, Arkansas, and First Baptist in Spartanburg, South Carolina, in 2005 and 2006, to build three church buildings in three of those poor communities. These Baptist churches would provide follow-up and also help to minister to over four hundred thousand people with the gospel of Jesus Christ. Many of the unbelievers were their families and friends who needed a personal relationship with Jesus Christ as their Lord and Savior. This would also help the gospel of Jesus Christ to be presented in the local schools and community centers, the local churches, and by door-to-door evangelism with many Southern Baptist folks of our Southern Baptist churches in America.

Bible studies would be started in the homes, and many times, this would provide a house church in the different communities that had no evangelical churches. In December of 2004, we were invited to celebrate Christmas with a precious Brazilian Baptist family in the city of Bocauva De Sol, Brazil, which was about twenty miles from Curitiba and near an area of over five hundred thousand people who did not know Jesus Christ as their personal Lord and Savior or did not have an evangelical church to worship in. These precious folks of the body of Jesus Christ would also help Janet and me to plant and start a new international Baptist community church in Bachacheri, a suburb of Curitiba. With over one and one half million foreigners who spoke English working in the Curitiba area, which has seven major automobile companies and four truck factories, God needed a place of worship in English that would become the mother church of many evangelical churches in the language of the people.

We were invited to the home of Lindiara Santana Santos and her husband, who lived on a ranch in the Bocaiúva Do Sol area. Sister Lindiara was the mayor of the community at God's design, and she would share her and God's vision for the gospel of Jesus Christ to be presented to the folks in that area with the prayers of many to have an Evangelical Baptist Church to worship Jesus Christ in.

Sister Edimara Santana Santos and her parents, Pastor Edir Felix dos Santos and his wife, Lindiomar Santana Santos, invited us to Lindiara's house for our first Christmas celebration in this area of Brazil.

We had been sent on a mission by our Lord Jesus Christ and the International Mission Board of the Southern Baptist Convention, and we joined our Lord Jesus Christ where He was already at work in the Curitiba, Brazil, area preparing the way for the gospel of Jesus Christ to save the lost people in this area and to help start Evangelical Baptist churches. Mayor Lindiara Santos shared with us the Lord's desire to start an Evangelical Baptist Church of the Brazilian Baptist Convention in this area of over five hundred thousand Brazilians who were unchurched and did not know the Lord Jesus Christ personally as their Lord and Savior.

Soon our Lord Jesus Christ revealed His desire to change the hearts of the people in Bocaiuva de Sol to me and to have them worship Him in Spirit and truth in a local church. Then with His will on my heart and life, I began to pray to bring a group of Southern Baptist volunteers to Bocauva de Sui to do mass evangelism in the homes and in the schools and to do a six-day crusade along with children's ministries. We would have the volunteers bring clothes, children's hygiene items, hair products to do haircuts and shampoos, toys, and some other items to meet the needs of these poor people. God also showed me that He had placed Mayor Lindiara Santos in office to become our Queen Esther of the Old Testament for such a time as this.

I then began to pray to the Lord Jesus Christ, asking who He wanted to use for this task and found that I was to ask my home Southern Baptist church in Taylorsville, North Carolina, led by Dr. Mike Runion, to bring a team of volunteers to help to start a new congregation of Brazilian Baptist folks in Portuguese.

Janet and I began to pray and to prepare for the team from Three Forks to come and to help start a mission Evangelical Baptist church, which would become the new mother church of the Baptist Evangelical churches in the area around Bocaiúva do Sol. This evangelical Baptist church would also be a mission church of the new International Community Baptist Church of Bacacheri, Curitiba, Brazil. The year 2005 would be another awesome year in our lives as we were serving with our Lord Jesus Christ in Curitiba, Brazil.

As Janet and I continued to advertise the International Community Church of Curitiba by placing our brochures in local hotels, businesses, and schools, we began to prepare through prayer for the first Sunday in March of 2005 to have our first worship service in the building provided by the mother church, Bacacheri Baptist Church. Dr. Luiz Roberto Silvado, the pastor, would also become my mentor and pastor as we served our Lord Jesus Christ under his ministry as pastors of the mother church of the new International Community Church of Curitiba. We also began a Wednesday night Bible study in English in Bacacheri for folks who were interested in a time of prayer and an English Bible study.

On the third night of our Wednesday night study, a Brazilian student who wanted to practice reading and hearing English came to our Bible Study. Soon he asked the question "How can I know God?" I then explained to him from God's Holy Word how he could know God personally as his Lord and Savior. After I explained to him that we were all sinners and needed to admit to Jesus Christ we needed His forgiveness and for Him to save us, the young man became a born-again follower and believer of our Lord Jesus Christ! Everyone in the Bible study was a believer and follower of Jesus Christ, and they welcomed him into the body of Christ.

As we prepared to have the first worship service of the new International Community Church of Curitiba, Brazil, on the first Sunday in March 2005, we continued to invite folks to join the new English church through many avenues in schools, hotels, businesses, bus terminals, and the major airport of Curitiba. Soon, the first worship service and Sunday school time of the new Purpose Driven Evangelical International Community was started with over fifty folks in Sunday school and over seventy present for the worship service. The Lord Jesus Christ also sent people to join our worship music team and the instruments needed to help lead the praise music for those present. It was an exciting time of watching Jehovah God grow His church and provide all of the needs of those who would become a part of His fellowship in this new English Evangelical Baptist church. The International Community Church of Curitiba, Brazil, would become the mother church of many Evangelical Baptist churches in this area of Brazil in the language of the people living in the area.

After the first worship service, people came to help grow the congregation with their love gifts, their tithes, their presence with their Spiritual gifts, and their joy of having a congregation who worshipped in English and were purpose-driven for our Lord Jesus Christ based on Baptist doctrines and practices. They came to worship as a congregation whose heartbeat was evangelism of the gospel of Jesus Christ, belief in the Word of God as all truth and inspired by the Holy Spirit of God as the author, and missions to win lost people of Curitiba, the state of Parana, the country of Brazil, and the nations of the world as true Acts 1:8 (NKJV) followers of Jesus Christ.

Soon International Mission Board Southern Baptist missionary Larry Murphy, serving as the leader of our Curitiba team of Southern Baptist international missionaries in Curitiba, Brazil, wrote a request to bring a Southern Baptist group of construction volunteers from First Baptist Church in Springdale, Arkansas, to build a new Baptist chapel. The local community near Curitiba were worshipping in a rented building, so now they were to have a Baptist chapel provided by our Lord Jesus Christ and His children from First Baptist Church in Springdale, Arkansas, to worship in.

During the days of the construction, another International Mission Board missionary Rick Thompson (now living and serving our Lord with his wife in Recipe, Brazil) and I would take members of the construction team visiting house to house to witness to folks and watch Jesus Christ change the hearts and lives of more than ten people in the community who would become new believers and followers of Jesus Christ. When the dedication service for the new chapel was held, there were over fifty people in the community and more than ten members of the construction team there and present to dedicate the new Brazilian Baptist church building for the glory of God. This would be an awesome experience for Janet and me since we were only construction helpers for the cause of Jesus Christ and His kingdom. Working shoulder to shoulder with many brothers in Christ who were over the age of sixty was awesome! This experience taught me that we could serve our Lord Jesus Christ as seniors in life.

During the months between May and August of 2005, volunteer teams from First Baptist, Springdale, Arkansas, and another Southern Baptist church from Florida came to do crusades and door-to-door evangelism in two other areas near Curitiba, Brazil, in answer to requests made by International Mission Board missionary Larry Murphy.

In each area, using a large circus tent, a medical bus, children's ministries during the day, crusades at night, and door-to-door personal evangelism, we witnessed the personal transformation of Brazilian people by the gospel of Jesus Christ. Over 130 folks would become believers and followers of our Lord Jesus Christ in each area, and a new evangelical Brazilian Baptist Church was started with a Brazilian Baptist church as the mother church to do follow-up visits and provide the pastor or leader for the new congregation.

On each occasion, Janet and I would also help provide translators for the teams and also join them in doing personal ministries during these times of helping to start new evangelical Brazilian Baptist churches. We would also mentor folks from the International Community Baptist Church of Curitiba by taking them with us to do ministries with the Southern Baptist volunteer teams from America. They would go house to house with Janet and me to translate in Portuguese and help to lead many folks to faith in Jesus Christ while using the tract *Steps to Peace with God*. This would also help those who would later answer God's call on their lives to serve Him in Brazil and around the world for Jesus Christ and His Kingdom, to be prepared to lead volunteer teams in the future for the cause of Jesus Christ. Janet and I were grateful for the Lord Jesus Christ allowing us to work with International Mission Board Southern Baptist missionaries in Brazil to learn the logistics of preparing for and planning for Southern Baptist teams to come to Brazil on mission with God. This training would help us to prepare for volunteer teams to come on mission with God everywhere we were serving with our Lord Jesus Christ.

As we were mentored and trained, we would also mentor and train national Christians and other International Mission Board Southern Baptist missionaries in how to prepare for volunteer teams and to allow those folks to experience a mighty movement of our Lord Jesus Christ in every country. We continued to watch our Lord grow His International Community Baptist Church of Curitiba, Brazil, during the first year of its life in 2005.

In the months of September through December 2005, members of the International Community

Church saw the need to prepare to begin a new Brazilian Baptist church in Bocaiuva do Sul. This was a small city in an area of over five hundred thousand folks who did not know Jesus Christ personally or have an evangelical Brazilian Baptist church. We began to prayer walk for the months leading up to a volunteer team from Three Forks Baptist Church in Taylorsville, North Carolina, who would come to do ministries in this area to help start a new evangelical Brazilian Baptist Church in Bocaiúva do Sul. Our Lord Jesus Christ had already been at work preparing the way by having a great Christian, Lindiara de Santos, elected as mayor of the city. This allowed the use of an area to place the large circus tent from First Baptist Curitiba, plus the medical bus to do children's ministries, door-to-door evangelism, talk to the children in the middle school, and do crusades at night.

Lindiara became our Queen Esther for such a time as this, and this opened up doors for our team to do ministries in September of 2006 in Bocaiuva do Sul, Brazil. By the end of 2005, in the International Community Church, the Lord had added many folks through first-time professions of faith in Jesus Christ and people from other denominations who were led by the Holy Spirit of God to join us in ministry. Our Thanksgiving and Christmas services brought many folks to worship with us and to celebrate with us a day of thanksgiving in November and our Lord Jesus Christ's birth. Over a hundred people attended each service. The meals were awesome, and we presented the folks present on Christmas Day crocheted crosses from a precious saint, Florence St. Clair, of Three Forks Baptist Church in Taylorsville, North Carolina. I was also able to do believers' baptismal services with the new believers who chose to follow Jesus Christ as their Lord and Savior.

Each volunteer team who came would also join our worship services and would preach, testify, and sing in English, which would bless the regular folks who came to worship God with us each Sunday and Wednesday night at our home Bible Study. We were using the book *Forty Days a Purpose Driven Life* and the Bible in English, which were given by the precious people of Three Forks Baptist Church. In addition, the precious congregation of First Baptist Church in Jonesboro, Arkansas, would send English Bibles for those who would worship with us in the International Community Church.

Many of those who joined us in worship would also send their family and friends who were living in other countries English Bibles so they could read and study about God's plan for their lives. We were told that many of these folks became followers and Believers in the Lord Jesus Christ.

In the year 2006, we and the folks of the International Community Church in Curitiba, Brazil, were to be witnesses to the work of our awesome God Jehovah in the lives of many in the Curitiba area. In the spring, a Baptist construction team from First Baptist Church of Spartanburg, South Carolina, came to build two Baptist chapels in twenty-one days in the poor communities in Curitiba. These poor new believers and followers of our Lord Jesus Christ were to receive new Baptist chapels in their areas so they could worship Jesus Christ and do ministries in their communities. Led by the International Mission Board missionary Bob Sarles (deceased), many on this team had helped to build from twenty-five to thirty Baptist chapels for new congregations in the southern to western area of Brazil. These new congregational meeting places were in poor places and would become lighthouses for the glory of our Lord Jesus Christ.

Janet and I prepared to receive a mission team from our home church, Three Forks Baptist Church in Taylorsville, the first of September of 2006 to help start a new mission Baptist Church in Bocaiuva do Sul, Brazil. We would lead our folks from the International Community Church on prayer walking events in Bocaiuva do Sul for three months before the Baptist team from Three Forks Baptist Church was to arrive in Curitiba. In addition, we would have preparation meetings with those who would be volunteer translators for those who were coming on mission with God to Curitiba from Three Forks and a sister Baptist church, East Taylorsville Baptist Church. Many on this team of ten had never been on a plane. In addition, many had never been out of the United States on either an airplane or other means of international travel, and they had never seen folks commit their lives for the first time by faith to Jesus Christ as their Lord and Savior. They brought with them many hygiene products, toys and games, and clothes for the poor people of Bocaiuva do Sul, both children and adults.

During the days, there were children's ministries done under a large circus tent, where washing hair, haircuts, and other hygiene acts were done for the children to show the love of Jesus Christ to those who would come. The team was also able to go into the middle school and do puppet ministries, play and sing southern gospel songs to those present, give out to each of the children personal hygiene products, and present the gospel of Jesus Christ to those present. At the end of the day, over three hundred students and teachers committed their lives for the first time to faith in Jesus Christ as their Lord and Savior.

During the six days of ministries going door to door during the day, almost ninety folks prayed to receive Jesus Christ as their Lord and Savior for the first time. Two of these people were on their deathbeds and their families and friends witnessed their confession of faith and belief in Jesus Christ as their Lord and Savior. They had assurance of what Jesus Christ said in John 14:1–6 (NKJV) and in John 14:12–14 (NKJV) that they had asked Jesus to forgive them of their sins and to save them and that they would be in heaven with Jesus Christ!

In addition, we would have them to read 1 John 5:9–13 (NKJV) and believe what the Word of God says. We especially highlighted verses twelve and thirteen:

> He who has the Son has life; he who does not have the Son of God does not have life. These things I have written to you who believe in the name of the Son of God, that you may know that you have eternal life, and that you may continue to believe in the name of the Son of God.

We would also have them read John 3:36 (NKJV), which says, "He who believes in the Son has everlasting life; and he who does not believe the Son shall not see life, but the wrath of God abides on him." When a new Believer and follower of Jesus Christ receives Jesus Christ as his or her Lord and Savior, he or she can trust and believe what the Word of God says and not believe by feelings or emotions. This was an awesome experience of the grace of God that changes people's lives when they believe by faith for all who were part of the mission experience. For the folks of Three Forks Baptist Church and the other sister Southern Baptist churches from the United States who had come on mission to Curitiba to help share the gospel of Jesus Christ and help start new evangelical Baptist churches, we were witnesses to what God could do and is doing in born-again believers for His glory!

As the year of 2006 was ending, since Janet and I had arrived in Curitiba, ten new evangelical churches were worshipping our Lord Jesus Christ in their communities and were autonomous evangelical Baptist churches planting new churches for the glory of God.

Each new congregation had a place to meet with a pastor leader to lead them in worship and personal service to and for our Lord Jesus Christ in their communities. Each congregation had a mother church that would help them in every area to grow those attending as true and real Acts 1:8 (NKJV) followers of our Lord Jesus Christ and for His kingdom. There were many believer's baptisms, as these new believers would follow the leadership of our Lord Jesus Christ and show those in their families and communities that they were part of God's born-again church.

God was at work in this area of Brazil, and we had the joy and honor to join Him there to experience a mighty movement of the Spirit of God in the lives of people.

As the year of 2007 began, I was invited to visit the local prison for boys and girls ages eleven through eighteen with local Baptist folks and Gideon leaders in Curitiba. Together, we would do worship services, give those prisoners the Word of God in Portuguese, and personally counsel those who asked to talk to us. After I shared my testimony of how Jesus had forgiven me of my sins and saved me from being a false religious leader of the Watchtower Society, I then preached from John 3:16 (NKJV), and fifty-four of these young men prayed to receive Jesus Christ as their Lord and Savior for the first time. Many also prayed to renew their commitment to Jesus Christ as their Lord and Savior and asked to study the Bible in a weekly Bible study held at the prison. This time was another awesome experience with our Lord Jesus Christ as He changed hearts and lives for His glory with these young boys. Many of the young girls also chose to follow Jesus Christ as their Lord and Savior and receive His Holy Word in their language. Follow-up visits each month helped all of these new followers of our Lord Jesus Christ be baptized (a large tub was used to do this in special worship services) and learn how to grow as a child of God in their personal lives and faith.

As the International Community Church of Curitiba continued to grow with many folks going on mission in Brazil and Paraguay to start new Baptist churches and watch many people receive Jesus Christ as their Lord and Savior, Joao Ricardo Morias became the associate pastor, and I mentored him for over two years so he could become the pastor and leader of the international community after Janet and I left to return to the United States and God's next assignment for our lives.

The Wednesday night Bible Study, using the Bible and Pastor Rick Warren's book *Forty Days a Purpose Driven Life*, witnessed one entire Brazilian family of seven become believers and followers of Jesus Christ. In addition, many more unbelievers in Jesus Christ would come to practice their English and commit their lives by faith in a personal relationship with Jesus Christ before we left Curitiba. Pastor Joao would continue this English Bible study after we left, and it continues to grow for Jesus Christ even today.

Many followed their first-time decision to follow Jesus Christ as their Lord and Savior with believer's baptism to show to their families, their friends, and their communities that they were true Acts 1:8 (NKJV) followers of their Lord Jesus Christ. Soon Janet and I were completing our three-year assignment with the International Mission Board in Curitiba in July of 2007 and returning to Taylorsville for the next chapter in our lives and ministries. We were invited by the Women's Missionary Union of Mt. Ruhama Baptist Church in Maiden, North Carolina, to live in their missionary home before we started the next chapter of our lives and ministries. In addition, we were invited to share our God stories and ministries in Brazil and South Korea in Global Mission conferences held in many of our Southern Baptist churches in different states.

After hearing the Spirit of God impressed on our hearts that we do not retire on Him and our calling to the nations, we contacted our International Mission Board to decide where our Lord was calling us to invest our lives and ministries. After much prayer, we asked to be the evangelists and church planters in Durban, South Africa, to fill that position and were accepted for that assignment. We were to go to the International Learning Center in Virginia to prepare for two weeks for the assignment in South Africa in May of 2008. Before that time, we were invited to do many Global Mission conferences in Southern Baptist churches of various cities and Baptist Associations around the South. These we did for God to be honored and glorified for what He was doing around the world for His kingdom.

Many people in the host homes that Janet and I would stay in at those churches we were being called to serve our Lord Jesus Christ as Acts 1:8 (NKJV) followers. Janet and I were used of our Lord to answer their questions and help the people know what to do in order to plan and to go on short- or long-term missions with other people going to the nations with our Lord. In addition, with them going with the Great Commission (Matthew 28: 18–20 NKJV) in their minds and on their hearts, people would be changed.

With Jesus Christ as our Lord and Savior, we will go into homes and restaurants, onto the streets, and into any place that God leads His followers to go. One young man received Jesus Christ, and his parents, his brother, and Janet were witnesses to his decision to follow Jesus Christ as his Lord and Savior. I was able to disciple him for three days. I was also present when he followed his decision to follow Jesus Christ with his life with the believer's baptism two months later at the age of seven years old. Before we left Curitiba, Brazil, and the International Community Church, we also had the joy and honor to commission two Brazilian Baptist families to Canada in answer to God's call on their lives to the nations. In addition, we found out that four families and three singles who were in our English Bible study were now serving in seven countries as international missionaries. It was a blessing to know that God had Janet and me to mentor these precious folks while we were serving our Lord in South Korea.

CHAPTER 8

We began the year of 2008 by traveling to meet with the International Mission Board of the Southern Baptist Convention in Richmond, Virginia, to read and look at evangelists' and church planters' assignments around the world. After much prayer over these assignments in many areas of the world, we believed in our hearts and in our spirits that God was calling us to Durban, South Africa, as evangelists and church planters.

After mission conferences at Southern Baptist Churches across the South, that spring, we witnessed many first-time professions of faith in Jesus Christ. We were also able to tell our God stories and show by DVD what our Lord was doing in many areas of the world where we had served with Him. Many of those host families that we stayed with were serving with our Lord Jesus Christ in many areas of the world for His glory and Kingdom. People, especially singles, would talk to Janet and me and ask us as how they could find out what people group God was calling them to for service. We would then tell them what steps they needed to take in order to find out God's will for their lives and ministries. We now know that many have followed up on their decisions to follow God's will with their lives. It is always a joy to be used by God to mentor those He is calling to go to the nations with the gospel of Jesus Christ.

We met some of them as we were again in training at the International Learning Center of the Southern Baptist convention in Rockville, Virginia, preparing to go to Durban, South Africa, to do evangelism and church planting before flying to South Africa in July of 2008.

It was a joy to learn about the Sub-Saharan people of South African and their culture and beliefs, as Janet and I would be living among them. This also included learning that there were thirteen different languages spoken among these people and that we would learn England's English and some Zulu and Afrikaans in order to share our faith. In addition, I could use my Portuguese (which I am fluent in speaking and understanding) to share with the Zulus. We would also use our English to share and to preach the whole counsel of God's Word.

We also had to learn to drive on the left-hand side of the road with the steering wheel on the right side of the car. We would change gears with our left hand, which was hard to get accustomed to. Many had been born there in Durban, South Africa.

We found a wonderful home, Umhlanga Beach, South Africa, to live in while doing ministries in an area near the Indian Ocean.

There were also seven troops of Berber monkeys living in our area, and sometimes they came into our home looking for food.

In the first ten months of our ministries in Durban and the surrounding areas, seven people came to know Jesus Christ personally as their Lord and Savior. One of these was a young graduate of the university in Johannesburg, South Africa, who was on vacation with her family in Durban.

In 2009, she sent us an email telling us that she had been baptized in a local evangelical church in London, England. She thanked us for introducing her to a personal relationship with Jesus Christ by faith at the Bible bookstore in the mall. She added that she was now teaching English using the Bible that the Lord had provided for her through our ministries, and she personally thanked us for praying with her and for her life as she served our Lord Jesus Christ in England. We also introduced two other folks in the coffee shop that we would visit each time we went to the South African mall in Durban, South Africa.

Janet and I would visit the mall to eat and to witness to folk, to help them to receive personal faith in Jesus Christ as their Lord and Savior. One of these people would become a witness to her family of God's love and grace through His son Jesus Christ, so that her entire family became true believers and followers of our Lord Jesus Christ. Many times, the Lord Jesus Christ would put me near folks to share with them what God had done in my life and that He loved them and would love to give to them a new life by faith in His Son Jesus Christ.

Janet and I were also used by our Lord to help start a new evangelical church that would meet in a local school building or in a home in the Zulu neighborhood. God grew this church to over twenty people in a short period of time, and we thanked our Lord for the hope He had given to many. In addition, I was asked to preach God's Holy Word in three evangelical Baptist churches in the area, where over one mission Indian immigrants were living.

In the first year of ministries in the Durban area, Janet and I witnessed fifteen people pray to receive Jesus Christ as their personal Lord and Savior at the services in Phoenix, Verulam, and Durban, South Africa. Praise the Lord! These folks used their decision to follow Jesus Christ with their lives with believer's baptism to show friends and families their personal decision of commitment to Jesus Christ through faith in Him. I had the joy and honor of helping to baptize them.

In the beginning of the year of 2009, Janet and I were asked to move to Johannesburg, South Africa, to do evangelism and church planting with the Soweto Evangelism team. In addition, we joined Krugersdorp Baptist Church to help minister to a group of folks who had been without a permanent pastor for a long time. We moved into the area to live and to serve with our Lord Jesus and the Soweto Evangelism team in an area near us. It was one of the communities that had over one million immigrants from eight different countries of Africa in the Johannesburg area. Many had come there to escape war, famine, and the disease of AIDS and to begin a new life. Their homes were small with no running water, bathrooms, or electricity. Many were hopeless and hurting. They did not believe that anyone cared about them. Our Soweto Evangelism team joined with the Baptist churches of the Baptist Union of South Africa in the Johannesburg, South Africa, area to help start new Evangelical Baptist churches. Our team would also start new churches in the Soweto community in the homes or in schools. Our team would go door to door every month in this area to share with the folks the love of Jesus Christ and to introduce them to a personal relationship with Him. We saw God save many people and help us to start two evangelical churches as we did follow-up with those who committed their lives to Jesus Christ by faith. In a short time, we witnessed over twenty people follow their decision to follow Jesus Christ with their lives with believer's baptism.

We started Bible studies to help grow these new believers in their faith and to help introduce their families who were not believers and followers of Jesus Christ to Jesus and encourage them to commit their lives by faith to Jesus Christ as their Lord and Savior. On one of these Saturdays in the Snake Park area of Soweto, my Lord used my story of salvation and faith in Jesus Christ to introduce two ex-Jehovah's Witnesses to faith in Jesus Christ as their Lord and Savior. This was an awesome experience for me. I watched Jesus Christ save them and give them hope and a new life by faith in Him. I could relate to these folk sand twenty-five other former Jehovah's Witnesses who were born again followers of Jesus Christ as their personal Lord and Savior. They were like me, new creations in Jesus Christ, who took their sin and gave to them His righteousness and life forever with Him.

Later during this time period of 2009, I was asked to preach and share my testimonies in two Baptist churches in this area of Soweto, and God blessed His Word because during invitation time, thirteen people committed their lives to Jesus Christ as their Lord and Savior. One of these new believers would be the local pastor's youngest daughter, whom the pastor would baptize the next week. The pastor's wife was very sick with a kidney problem but was able to attend her daughter's baptism service. This was a very special time in the pastor's family and church family as they witnessed eight new believers receive the believer's baptism to show that they were going to follow Jesus with their lives.

In the fall of 2009, in another local Evangelical Baptist church that we were attending near our home, we had a wonderful Sunday morning worship service where God showed up! In this service, the pastor and I were asked by five people to pray the prayer of faith over them so that God could heal them in His way and time. One man was scheduled for surgery on a large tumor the following Tuesday, but when the medical people took x-rays of the area before surgery, the tumor was gone! The other folks who were prayed over also had their prayers answered with God's special healing! Our Lord is still in the healing work for His glory!

Soon, we were notified by our family that our oldest daughter, Angela Brown, was diagnosed with kidney cancer, and Janet and I took medical leave to go home for her surgery. We returned to South Africa with heavy hearts for her and her family. God began to close doors of ministries for us, but we were faithful to continue to serve Him until He told us it was time to go home. We soon received word that other members of our family were going through cancer treatments, and our youngest daughter was going through a divorce with two sons at the university, studying for their degrees. God so broke our hearts over these problems in our families that we finally heard His voice to go home and minister to our families. Therefore, we resigned from the International Mission Board and our assignment in South Africa to return to Taylorsville, North Carolina, to serve our Lord Jesus Christ in the next chapter of our lives and ministries. This chapter in our lives would include both home and international ministries. In addition, Janet and I would share in mission conferences with many of our Southern Baptist churches in America.

God would also have me preach revivals and renewals in many Southern Baptist churches in Virginia, North Carolina, and South Carolina. As I always shared my personal story of how Jesus Christ saved me and that I am a born-again (Acts 1:8 NKJV) follower of our Lord Jesus Christ, many folks committed their lives by faith to Jesus Christ as their Lord and Savior.

We arrived back in Taylorsville, North Carolina, on February 2, 2010, and began to pray for a place to live and furniture since we did not have either because Jehovah God had provided where we stayed since 1995. Soon God would bless us with a home and furniture, and Janet could help Angela every time she needed help to go to the hospital or to the different doctors both in our area and other cancer centers for her treatments. We would become active in our local Three Forks Baptist Church, using our gifts and ministries.

Janet would soon become involved in the Women's Missionary Union of Three Forks and eventually their leader. We would also remind the precious folk of Three Forks that we were representing both our Lord Jesus Christ and them as their resident missionaries. In addition, I would be a volunteer Sunday school teacher wherever I was needed when we were not gone serving our Lord with His call on our lives.

Soon I was asked to go with a volunteer team from Three Forks Baptist Church led by Brother Donnie Rogers and his wife, Vicki Rogers. I was asked to preach, to give the time for commitment to a personal believing faith in Jesus Christ, and to help teach during vacation Bible studies in the mission evangelical churches and orphanages. I joined the team led by Donnie and Vicki Rogers with Glenda Chapman, Sina Brown, Randy Gilliland, and Kevin Taylor to do vacation Bible school in churches and in orphanages and to share our faith and love of Jesus Christ with the folks in and around Novgorod, Russia.

I was also asked to share my testimony and to teach how to share the gospel of Jesus Christ with Jehovah's Witnesses with twenty-two pastors and congregations. I spoke about the beliefs and practices of the Watchtower Society. They were taught to trust the Holy Spirit of God to lead in a witnessing encounter instead of trying to do in the flesh what only the Holy Spirit of God could do. I also taught them and all believers in Jesus Christ as their Lord and Savior to share their personal testimony of where they were before they met Jesus Christ, what happened after they met Jesus Christ as their personal Lord and Savior, and where they were at that time in Jesus Christ, trusting Him as their Lord and Savior. I always teach God's children that if you are a born-again follower and believer in Jesus Christ as your Lord and Savior, then no one can deny what you have personally experienced, not even the evil one himself. I also teach that we must leave the results in the lives of lost people to God, but we can pray that they meet the real Lord Jesus Christ as we have through faith and trusting in Him. Only God can see their hearts. Unless the Holy Spirit of God draws lost people to Jesus Christ, they will not confess and believe that He is Lord and Savior.

I was asked to teach 151 students in the vacation Bible school held in Three Forks Baptist Church. On the day of my teaching and reading to these precious children John 3:16 (NKJV), after I explained the fact that one must be born again from above by our Heavenly Father in order to be with Jesus in heaven, seven of these precious children prayed to receive Jesus Christ as their Lord and Savior. They followed this personal decision with believer's baptism by being immersed in water one month later to show their families and friends as well as the world that they were following Jesus Christ with their lives.

Our first vacation Bible school after arriving in Novgorod, Russia, was held at a mission church, the Temple of the Holy Trinity in Chechulino, Russia, led by Pastor Sergei. God moved in a mighty way in the hearts and lives of those who came for the four-day vacation Bible study time. In the morning time, the young Russian boys and girls would come to do crafts, hear, read, and study the Holy Bible in Russian and do recreation time. In the afternoon, the older Russian boys and girls would come to do crafts, read a true Bible story, and also do recreation time. The time together would also include an assembly time, where a drama would be acted out. They would learn songs to sing as well as hear a short Bible sermon. The children were also to learn twelve Bible verses by memory and quote them back to the members of the local congregation in order to win a great prize. The children were to draw by memory a picture of one of the Bible stories with those chosen as the winners to receive gifts.

I was asked to teach the older boys' classes of fifty-four boys, ages ten to twenty-one years of age. The classes were divided into three with the oldest class being ages fourteen to twenty-one. Many of these young boys had never had a Bible to read or ever seen a man of God my age, as I was sixty-seven years old this first time there. I would tell the Bible stories after having the boys read the passage of Holy Scripture each day. It helped them to hear the Word of God as the verses were read for the first time and then to hear the Word of God as I spoke to them.

On the fourth day, as I was using the gospel tract *Steps to Peace with God* in Russian, all fifty-four boys prayed out loud for the first time to ask Jesus Christ to forgive them of their sins and to save them! During commitment time with all of the children in Chechulino present, over ninety children prayed for the first time to receive Jesus Christ as their Lord and Savior! What a blessing to all who witnessed these decisions because it brought glory and honor to our Lord Jesus Christ and His kingdom. Our next place to do vacation Bible school was a community orphanage about twenty-five miles southeast of Novgorod, Russia.

Many of these children were born in the community, but their mothers could not support their needs, so they lived in the orphanage. Their mothers also came to the orphanage when we arrived to do vacation Bible school. Many of these folk would hear the gospel of Jesus Christ for the first time plus receive a Russian Bible.

During the Bible story time one day, six children and two mothers made a first-time commitment of faith in Jesus Christ as their Lord and Savior. As we would do in every place at the end of our time, we had each child "go fish" to receive a bag of toys and hygiene products. Many of these bags had been prepared before our time in Russia by Glenda Chapman, and the children and adults were blessed to receive them. In addition to these bags, the children were given a Russian Bible (either a Children's Bible or a King James Version both in Russian), a bag of cookies, a banana, a juice drink, and a Russian Snickers candy bar.

Our next vacation Bible school was done in an evangelical church and an orphanage near the church about thirty miles southwest of Novgorod, Russia. The orphanage had many beautiful children who were ready to receive the team with beautiful smiles and joy on their faces. Many of these children were hungry for love and affection from the team and excited to hear our Bible story about a Savior named Jesus Christ, whose love we had brought with us for those children and teachers to see and experience. Three of these children who understood the gospel of Jesus Christ when it was explained to them from God's Holy Word prayed to receive Jesus Christ by faith as their personal Lord and Savior. These children and teachers received the gifts and food with gratitude and joy.

In the local evangelical church, children and adults also received the good news about Jesus Christ with a personal commitment by faith in Him for forgiveness of their sins and salvation for their souls. Ten of these people prayed to receive Jesus Christ as their personal Lord and Savior, with their pastor and congregation committing to help grow these new believers in their faith and to baptize them soon into the body of Christ. This was a spiritual high for both the team and the local believers in Jesus Christ as their Lord and Savior.

After our team had left to return to the mother Evangelical church in Novgorod, Russia, we were asked to do a conference on how to witness to Jehovah's Witnesses and to teach about what they profess to believe. As I led this conference, which included telling my personal born-again experience with Jesus Christ, I explained what the Watchtower Society taught and believed, which changes every year. The more than twenty congregations had time to ask me questions about my conversion experience, my family, and my ministries as an international Southern Baptist minister since being born again. In addition, during this time, a young teenage lady heard me explaining how my God had put Janet in my life as my wife and partner in ministries to teach me how to pray, to start the day with my Lord with a devotion time and reading the Bible, and to pray with a prayer list for all those who needed to know Jesus Christ as their personal Lord and savior. On the last Sunday before returning home to North Carolina, we worshipped in the mother church in Novgorod, and the young lady came with one of my translators to give me a letter for Janet. She then asked me to ask Janet to be a part of her life and asked that Janet would become a prayer warrior for her and her life.

As the team prepared to return to Taylorsville, North Carolina, we reflected on the experiences and the lives that we saw Jesus Christ change during our time in Russia. Over one hundred and fifty new believers and followers of Jesus Christ as their Lord and Savior were born again. The orphanages and churches were encouraged to hear what our God was doing around the world as Lord, and our hearts and 155 lives were changed. We were all burdened to pray for the folks in Novgorod and in Russia to know by faith and personally Jesus Christ as their Lord and Savior.

After returning home, Janet and I were invited to many Global Mission conferences in 2010 to represent the International Mission Board as global international Southern Baptist missionaries. We were also able to minister to our daughter Angela Brown's family as she battled kidney cancer and its terrible effect on her body and life. It was a joy to be a caregiver for her; her husband, Steve; and her sons, Jeremy Brown and Austin Williams, and his family. This also allowed us time to spend with our daughter Tracy Chapman and her sons, Eric and Shawn, and encourage and minister to this precious family. In addition, we were also able to be near and to encourage our son Ryan Burns and his family, who live in Charlotte, North Carolina, and worship and serve our Lord Jesus Christ as members of Carmel Baptist Church in Charlotte, North Carolina.

Our first Global Missions Conference was in Englewood Baptist Church in Rocky Mount, North Carolina. There, we were used to thank the folk for giving to the Lottie Moon Christmas Offering for our International Mission Board Southern Baptist missionaries and to share our God stories that took place in South Africa, Brazil, Russia, and South Korea. As we shared with the seniors of Englewood Baptist Church, called "Prime Timers," other missionaries also shared with those of us who were there what God was doing in the lives of born-again Jehovah's Witnesses in their areas of the world. In addition, one of the missionaries serving with the Wycliffe Bible Translators also shared a personal testimony of being born again after many years as one of Jehovah's Witnesses. This was an awesome God time that encouraged me and those present with how Jesus

Christ was changing the lives of Jehovah's Witnesses around the world to be born again. They would become real (Acts 1:8 NKJV) followers of our Lord Jesus Christ.

In fact, I have also met many born-again Jehovah's Witnesses who are now going as Christ's witnesses in North America and around the world to share their life-changing story of faith in Jesus Christ as their Lord and Savior.

The next mission conference at which we were used to tell our God stories was with the Appomattox Baptist Association of Appomattox, Virginia. Our host Southern Baptist church was New Chapel Baptist Church in Rustburg, Virginia, where Janet and I were hosted by two of God's children. These two precious children of our Lord fed us with mouthwatering home cooking and ministered to our needs while we were there to serve our Lord Jesus Christ with them and their congregation. The Lord changed lives during the worship services, and we also thanked the congregation for giving to the Lottie Moon offering at Christmastime so that we could go in answer to God's call on our lives to be His witnesses to the nations. Janet and I were loved by the people of New Chapel Baptist Church and the Appomattox Baptist Association and enjoyed our time with God's family there in Appomattox, Virginia. For the rest of 2010, we were used in Southern Baptist Churches, including Mountain View Baptist Church in Hickory, North Carolina, where our Lord had the Sunday school class that we were assigned to share with witness God heal a lady of breathing problems. As we anointed her and prayed over her the prayer of faith, which is found in James 5:13–16 (NKJV), she began to feel better.

We were next blessed by our Lord Jesus Christ as we shared our God stories with the folks of Mount Pleasant, Baptist Church in Carrollton, Georgia. God was honored, and Jesus was lifted up high in all of the services.

After this time, we were with First Baptist Church in Spartanburg, South Carolina, and then Cape Carteret Baptist Church in Cape Carteret, North Carolina. Next was Woolsey Baptist Church in Fayetteville, Georgia, and then Glen Hope Baptist Church in Burlington, North Carolina. In every Baptist church, Jesus was lifted up high, and He changed lives, including ours, for His glory and His kingdom. We concluded the year of 2010 with mission conferences in First Baptist Church Darlington, South Carolina; Bethel Baptist Church in Ronda, North Carolina; First Baptist Church in Collinsville, Virginia; Draytonville Baptist Church in Gaffney, South Carolina; and Pleasant Hill Baptist Church in Martin, Georgia. In each conference, God showed up in a mighty way and changed hearts and lives, including Janet's and mine. What a mighty God we serve! We also understand that when you honor Him with your life, He will honor you. *Amen*! We also gave thanks to our God and Lord that even though our daughter Angela Brown had a very trying year in battling the kidney cancer, which had spread to other parts of her body, she rejoiced as a winner because her Lord had gotten her through another year, and she was able to celebrate Thanksgiving and Christmastime with her family. Angela continued to shine for her Lord Jesus Christ and became a bright light for Jesus Christ as she ministered to everyone who was ministering to her and her family with the love of Jesus Christ!

CHAPTER 9

The year 2011 began with me traveling to Rockdale Baptist Church in Conyers, Georgia, to do a Global Missions Conference and then to Northside Baptist Church in West Columbia, South Carolina, where Janet and I were able to share our God stories with those folks. In each congregation, we were able to watch Jesus Christ change many lives with folks saying yes to His invitation for salvation and folks saying yes to God's call to be missionaries to the nations (four couples and two singles said yes to God's call on their lives). We then went to Utica Baptist Church in Seneca, South Carolina, and to Colonial Baptist Church in Randallstown, Maryland, to share with those folks about what our Lord was doing around the world for His kingdom. We then were used in Global Mission Conferences in Tri Cities Baptist Church in Gray, Tennessee; North Point Baptist Church in Weaverville, North Carolina; and Grace Baptist Church in Fayetteville, North Carolina, prior to preaching a revival in First Baptist Church in Collinsville, Virginia. Many folks prayed to receive Jesus Christ as their Lord and Savior for the first time during these God assignments for us.

In June of 2011, I was a member of Three Forks Baptist Church Russia team with Donnie and Vicky Rogers, Delores Fox, Glenda Chapman, Randy Gilleland, and Kevin Taylor. We traveled to Novgorod, Russia, on a mission with our Lord Jesus Christ. Every member served our Lord with doing crafts, reading Bible stories, overseeing recreation time, and giving away gifts, Russian Bibles, and food in each church and orphanage that we did vacation Bible study services with. We were able to witness over 120 children plus adults pray for the first time to receive Jesus Christ as their personal Lord and Savior. In addition, Randy, Delores, Glenda, Vicky, and Donnie Rogers had a craft teaching tea and sweet food time with the ladies of the different evangelical churches at the mother evangelical church in Novgorod, Russia. These precious ladies were blessed by learning how to make straw baskets and other crafts for their homes and to sell for extra income for their families. Kevin Taylor would provide music in all of the services that we did and help in every area where he was needed!

Each person in the group would either sing or testify about his or her faith story, and I would preach and give a personal invitation after each service and Bible story time. Donnie Rogers would always share first to thank the folk for inviting us to come and to do ministry with them because of the love of Jesus Christ in our hearts. At the conclusion time, this would become a personal time for folks to receive Jesus Christ as their personal Lord and Savior, to join with the local evangelical fellowship to share the love and grace of our Lord Jesus Christ, and to give to those present the opportunity to recommit their lives to Jesus Christ as their Lord and Savior. This team was anointed by our Lord to make a difference in every person's life while serving with their gifts and talents, and I believe in my heart that Jehovah God was pleased and honored with the glory that He received. All of us witnessed God do miracles and change hearts and lives as people received Jesus Christ as their personal Savior and Lord. Many learned how to do crafts that they could make and sell to help their families to have extra income for their needs.

The rest of the year of 2011 was blessed with Janet and I doing many Global Missions Conferences in our sister Southern Baptist churches in the South. We enjoyed our opportunities for ministries with Sunday school classes and the folks of God's church in the First Baptist Church of Spartanburg, South Carolina; First Baptist Church of Jonesville, Virginia; the Heights Baptist Church of Colonial Heights, Virginia; Richland Community Church of Wake Forest, North Carolina; Bethlehem Baptist Church of Simpsonville, South Carolina; and Halesford Baptist Church of Wirtz, Virginia.

In each church, we were able to share our God stories concerning our service with our Lord Jesus Christ in Brazil, South Korea, South Africa, and Russia. We would witness many folks say yes to God's call on their lives to His ministry, His call to the nations, and for personal salvation through faith and trust in Jesus Christ as their Lord and Savior. Janet and I also were blessed by renewing fellowship with the children of a family whom we served with on the island of Cheju, South Korea. We were invited to the Global Missions Conference held in North Pointe Baptist Church in Weaverville, North Carolina, and the young ladies were members there. They were both in Mars Hill University, and because they were both young girls the last time that we had seen them, we rejoiced in who they had become in Jesus Christ.

In each congregation that we shared our testimonies, our God stories, and what our Lord Jesus Christ was doing around the world, we witnessed many come to saving faith in Jesus Christ. Also many folks, young and old, would talk to us about their call from God to go to the nations, and we would help them begin to seek the next chapter of their lives for Jesus Christ. In addition, many people would talk to me about a call from God to serve Him with the rest of their lives in ministry. I would suggest to them that if they could do anything else with their lives but serving our living Lord, they needed to do that. However, if they had no peace about their decision, then they needed to surrender to His will and call on their lives. I would share what it took for me to say yes to God and to tell Him not my will but yours for my life. I then would suggest to them what they needed to do to prepare their lives to serve Him as the best servant that they could be and then do it.

The year of 2012 would prove to be another awesome year for us, as Janet served our home church as the Women's Missionary Union leader, helping the children and adults have a vision of serving our Lord Jesus Christ in missions and doing evangelism for Jesus Christ, and I would do many mission conferences with Southern Baptist churches and go on missions to Novgorod, Russia. God would use Janet in ministries for our children in Three Forks and across the South with young girls and women for His glory and honor. As she was both an international Southern Baptist missionary and a home missionary for the Southern Baptist Convention, God would use her to tell her God experiences around the world. They would always include her personal encounter with Jesus Christ as an almost nine-year-old child. In addition, Janet and I were caregivers to our daughter Angela Brown and her family as she continued to battle kidney cancer in her body. It was a joy and an honor to us.

In the spring of 2012, I went to do a Global Mission Conference with the people of the First Baptist Church of Douglasville, Georgia. It was an awesome time of sharing my testimony on the programs with the current president of the Southern Baptist Convention and the past president of the Southern Baptist Convention.

After each service and the breakout sessions on ministering to Jehovah's Witnesses, one young man talked to me about God's call on his life to preach His Word. After sharing with him my call and preparation to serve our Lord Jesus Christ with the rest of my life, I introduced him to the current president of New Orleans Baptist Theological Seminary, who helped him to get started with his preparation to serve our Lord Jesus Christ.

Another personal experience was with a young university graduate who knew that God was calling her to the mission field as an Acts 1:8 (NKJV) follower around the world. We helped her to begin her preparation with the International Mission Board of the Southern Baptist Convention, who would help her to discover where our Lord Jesus Christ was leading her to serve. In addition, the personal driver of the First Baptist Church of Douglasville assigned to drive me where I was needed and his wife had just said yes to God's call on their lives as North American Mission Board missionaries. He was fifty-one. He told me how much of an encouragement it was to him to hear how God had used me the last twenty years, as I also started late in life as one of His missionaries.

During the breakout sessions, while I was teaching on how to witness to Jehovah's Witnesses, many folks would come to tell me that they had family and friends who were Jehovah's Witnesses, and they were grateful to hear how Jesus Christ had forgiven and saved me. My story had encouraged them to pray for their friends and families, asking Jesus Christ to save them. This would always happen in every evangelical and Southern Baptist church that I would share with. In addition, when I would give a personal invitation to those present to come to faith in Jesus Christ as their personal Lord and Savior, I witnessed many receive Jesus Christ as their personal Lord and Savior by faith.

It was soon time to prepare to return to Novgorod, Russia, on a mission for Jesus Christ with the team from Three Forks Baptist Church, led by Donnie Rogers. With Donnie and Vicky Rogers were Randy Gilleland (a member of Mount Herman Baptist Church in Taylorsville, North Carolina), Kevin Taylor, and I. We went to do ministries in orphanages and local evangelical churches in Novgorod and surrounding cities. We spent the first day and night in St. Petersburg, Russia, shopping for the items to use in the vacation Bible school ministries in the different cities, evangelical churches, and orphanages for our Lord Jesus Christ to add to His church with the cost being cheaper than it was in America. We also were allowed to sleep in the beds of the Baptist Seminary of Russia in St. Petersburg at a small cost to each of us. Our translators, who had come to receive us, were too.

This time proved to be a blessing to me, as I met many Russian Baptist students who were preparing to serve our Lord Jesus Christ in different places in Russia. I was able to encourage and to mentor them as they were beginning a new chapter in their lives. I was able to give them a Word from God (Jeremiah 29:11) (NKJV) and to pray with them and for them to just be faithful to God's call on their lives and let Him do His work in the lives of the people they would minister to. This was a great lesson that I had learned from our Lord in North Carolina as the pastor of our first mission church.

The next day, we traveled to Novgorod, Russia, to begin our ministries using Southern Baptist vacation Bible school materials with the mission churches and orphanages in the southeast area of Russia. By the end of the ministry time in these areas where we were doing vacation Bible studies, preaching and teaching the Word of God, and witnessing about the love and grace of God found only in a personal relationship with Jesus Christ, over one hundred people were added to the family of Jesus Christ. We were also able to do Bible conferences with the local pastors and their congregations to encourage them with the Word of God.

While I was with the Three Forks Russia team in Russia, Janet was able to fly to Curitiba, Brazil, on a mission to help meet with many of the ten Evangelical Brazil Baptist churches that we had helped to start while we served there with our Lord Jesus Christ and the International Mission Board of the Southern Baptist Convention as Masters Plus Missionaries. She was able to thank them for their ministries for our Lord and for us and to help them to know that our Lord was using us to serve Him since we had left Brazil. Janet was able to stay with her sister in Christ Amariles Lustosa (who lives in Curitiba, Brazil), and together, they would visit the different Baptist churches to give to the folks an encouraging word from our Lord Jesus Christ. Janet was also able to teach and to speak in the international school that Amariles owned and to help minister to Amariles while staying with her in the apartment above the school. Our Lord also used Janet for His glory and name as she flew to Curitiba, Brazil, and returned to Charlotte, North Carolina, with folks on the planes and in the different airports.

I next went to Tompkinsville, Kentucky, to do a Global Mission Conference with the Monroe Baptist Association, where God blessed many areas of ministry. The first Sunday during the personal invitation to come to Jesus Christ in faith, a young lady came forward to ask Jesus Christ into her life and to forgive her and save her. Everyone there rejoiced with her personal decision to follow Jesus Christ with her life, and the lady who would clean my room where we were staying told me that afternoon that the young lady was her daughter and had led a heartbroken life, but Jesus had healed her, cleansed her, and made her a new creation.

On that Sunday night, a young man came forward during invitation time to surrender to God's call to preach His Word and tell the pastor and the congregation so they could pray for him, as he would begin to prepare to serve our Lord Jesus Christ with his life. Another person came to commit their life to Jesus for the first time, asking Him to forgive them and to save them and become their personal Lord and Savior. Other folks came for renewal of their commitment to Jesus Christ and to become a part of the fellowship and serve Jesus there.

On Monday, the fifteen local missionaries from the North American Mission Board, representing the United States and Canada, and the International Mission Board, representing many countries and cultures invited us to four different local elementary schools to share about the different cultures and countries that we were serving or had served in. We were able to show on the international maps or globes where we had lived or were living in now and to help the children to learn about the different languages, food, and living conditions. In addition, we were able to answer their questions about why we would leave America to go and to live with the different groups in other countries.

On Monday, Tuesday, and Wednesday nights, all of the missionaries were in different Baptist Churches in Tompkinsville, Kentucky, preaching and sharing what God was doing around the world for His name's sake.

On Tuesday morning, all the missionaries were invited to three middle schools in Tompkinsville to meet the children and to share about the different cultures in the different countries that we had lived in. On Wednesday morning, we all were invited to the local high school to meet the students and to share our experiences with them. These times with the students also allowed us to mentor them, encourage them with the love of Jesus Christ, and let them ask us questions. In each Baptist Church that my Lord allowed me to tell my story of salvation and His call on my life for the rest of the time here on this earth, many who heard my story said yes to God's call on their lives.

This conference was also a time for me to be encouraged and for my spirit and soul to be renewed and blessed. When the conference was over, all of the missionaries left to return to their place of service with a renewed spirit and the joy of the Lord in their lives. Each of us had witnessed God at work in Tompkinsville, Kentucky, as He changed lives and renewed the lives of His appointed servants.

In September of 2012, our daughter Angela finished her fight with kidney cancer and went home to be with her Lord Jesus Christ to receive her new body. We rejoice in celebration for her even though we miss her because we know that because of her trust and faith in Jesus Christ, we are only separated from her by time and space. Why? Both her mother and I have the same faith and trust in our Lord Jesus Christ and His promises in John 14:1–6 (NKJV). We will see her again with those saints who belong to God's family.

Janet and I finished 2012 doing mission conferences and sharing what our Holy God was doing around the world. We thank our Lord for who He is and what He has done and continues to do in our lives as He uses us for His glory and honor!

Soon, we would be beginning a new year of service to Him in 2013. We would watch and witness His miracles in changing people's lives through faith in Him. Janet and I began the year of 2013 with Global Missions Conferences in West Columbia, South Carolina, at Northside Baptist Church. We were able to share our God stories in Sunday school classes and also in the worship services. Our time with these folks was awesome, as we were able to testify as to how Jesus Christ saved us and called us to serve Him with our lives as true Acts 1: 8 (NKJV) followers of Jesus. We also witnessed folks turn to Jesus Christ by faith in Him and follow Him with their obedient lives wherever He would lead them.

Next, we were in Piedmont, South Carolina, in Community Fellowship church, a new Southern Baptist Church, telling our God stories to these folk.

We were able to encourage many whose desire was to be faithful and obedient servants of our Lord Jesus Christ with our personal testimonies and ministries on four continents and in sixteen nations with our Lord Jesus Christ. After our personal time with the folks of Connection Fellowship Church in Piedmont, South Carolina, I prepared to again go on a mission with the mission team from Three Forks Baptist Church to Novgorod, Russia. Donnie and Vicky Rogers, Kevin Taylor, Randy Gilleland, and I were excited to once again share our faith and love for our Savior Jesus Christ with the Russian folks in five evangelical churches and do vacation Bible school with two orphanages and three churches.

During these times, over 150 children and adults became believers and followers of our Lord Jesus Christ! Praise the Lord! Sharing and showing the love of Jesus Christ to these folks was both a joy and a blessing to each of us as our Lord Jesus Christ showed us His love. His awesome Holy Spirit drew unbelievers in Jesus Christ to Jesus by faith in Him in a way that we could see and witness His grace and faithfulness to our efforts in ministries. After we returned to Taylorsville, North Carolina, I soon left to travel to Scott Depot, West Virginia, near Ridley, West Virginia, to be one of the visiting Southern Baptist missionaries during the West Virginia Southern Baptist children's camp there. I shared my testimony of my personal faith in Jesus Christ as my Lord and

Savior and taught on cross-cultural ministries and preaching during the worship services at night. At the end of the week, four young Girls in Action and Royal Ambassadors ages six to ten committed their lives by faith in becoming believers and followers of Jesus Christ as their Lord and Savior.

In addition, during the worship services for the young boys and girls, ages twelve to eighteen, three committed their lives to faith in Jesus Christ as their Lord and Savior, and two came forward to say yes to God's call on their lives to go as His missionaries to the nations in obedience to Him. This camp proved to be an awesome time for those present and for the local community as vacation Bible schools were done with the local folks. There were also clown ministries put on by a wonderful evangelical team of students from North Greenville University located in Greenville, South Carolina. Two of these students also said yes to God's call on their lives to follow Him in obedience to go to the nations as His Acts 1:8 (NKJV) missionaries, representing Southern Baptists as International Missionaries of the Southern Baptist Convention. This time of ministry was a blessing to my spirit, as I both taught on how Jesus saved me with my personal testimony from a false religious leader as one of Jehovah's Witnesses and how my Lord had used me and my service to Him on many continents.

After I finished my awesome time in West Virginia, Janet and I went to do a Global Missions Conference in the First Baptist Church in Rock Hill, South Carolina. It was there that I was asked to introduce the speaker before the Wednesday night worship service. What a blessing that was to me because I was saved during the Christmas cantata, which our speaker, as the music minister of Long Leaf Baptist Church in Wilmington, North Carolina, was leading. I had not seen this special minister of music in over twenty years and to be able to worship with both him and his wife, who also sang in the cantata, was a blessing to Janet and me. My son Ryan Burns was also present in the congregation to hear my testimony of my salvation and how much I was blessed by his life, which God used to show me my need for Jesus Christ to forgive me of my sins and to trust Him by faith.

After a short personal testimony of my faith and trust in Jesus Christ as my Lord and Savior, I introduced the guest speaker to the congregation. He gave a personal invitation to those present to come to Jesus Christ for forgiveness and salvation and four folks came by faith to receive Jesus Christ. They each prayed out loud to Jesus, asking Him to forgive them and to save them, and they would turn from their sin to follow Him with their lives for the rest of their lives. God was honored and blessed. Plus, four new lives were written down in the Lamb's (Jesus Christ's) book of life.

After preaching from the book of Acts, the speaker shared God's Word and a call to repentance and renewal for those present, "thus saith the Lord," to all who heard. Janet and I were blessed with our time with the Bible study groups as we shared what God was doing around the world for His Name and His kingdom. Plus during the men's get together at a local farm, we were fed and allowed to play golf, swim in a pond, and meet all who came and their children. I talked to one blessed brother in Christ about how he could share his faith with a close friend who was one of

Jehovah's Witnesses. A few months later, he contacted me and told me that this man had become a follower and a believer in Jesus Christ as His Lord and Savior.

Janet also shared with the ladies of First Baptist, Rock Hill, South Carolina, her testimony of faith in Jesus Christ as a young girl of eight and a half and how she grew up as a member of Penelope Baptist Church in Hickory, North Carolina, involved in the missions program. In addition, she shared how God had prepared her to go to the nations of the world as an international missionary of the Southern Baptist Convention by allowing her to go on missions with members of Penelope to West Virginia to witness, do backyard Bible clubs, and help start Evangelical Baptist churches in the Wheeling, West Virginia, area of the United States. This mission conference really blessed our lives, and we believe that Jesus was lifted up high and our God was honored.

I next flew to Springfield, Illinois, to do another On Mission Celebration with the Capital City Baptist Association of Springfield, Illinois, and surrounding areas. My host family was the pastor of Havana Southern Baptist Church of Havana, Illinois, and his wife. These folks were so sweet to host me and to feed me with wonderful meals. God blessed me during the services in every Southern Baptist church that I spoke in while I was there. Besides Havana Southern Baptist Church, I did services with First Baptist Church of Petersburg, Illinois; New Life Baptist Church in Athens, Illinois; and Mt. Zion Baptist Church in Melbourne, Illinois. I was also able to share with all of the Southern Baptist churches in the Capital City Baptist Association during a mission fair held in Chatham Baptist Church in Chatham, Illinois. During the mission fair, each of the many missionaries, both local and international, set up a mission table with items representing the different people groups that the missionaries represented.

Since Janet and I had served with five different people groups on this earth with our Lord Jesus Christ as International Mission Board Masters Plus Missionaries of the Southern Baptist Convention, we had items from North America, Brazil, South Korea, South Africa, and Russia to show the folks who visited our tables. In addition, we were introduced personally to those folks present for the opening worship service with over twenty Southern Baptist churches represented. We were allowed ten to fifteen minutes to share our God stories about what our Heavenly Father was doing around the world with these precious people who gave so all of us could go where Jesus Christ had called us to go.

Before the On Mission Celebration began, as was done in every On Mission Celebration that Janet and I had done, the missionaries, along with young boys and girls from the association, marched in holding a flag representing a certain country that had Evangelical Southern Baptist missionaries on assignment with our Lord and the leadership of the Southern Baptist Convention of the International Mission Board. Before the On Mission Celebration worship service for the entire local Baptist association, there would be an awesome meal, either prepared by local members of the different congregations or catered. Many of those folks from the local congregations of the different Baptist associations that had these On Mission Celebrations would come and bring visitors to meet and talk to the different missionaries. Besides the worship services, Sunday school classes would host the missionaries in their classes on Sunday mornings and host them in one of the homes or in a restaurant for a time of fellowship and sharing. I was invited to join a men's interdenominational Bible study held weekly in Havana Southern Baptist Church. This was a great time of worship and fellowship with the body of Christ. The pastor of Havana Baptist Church and I also joined with one of his deacons in visiting his mother, who was a nonbeliever and not a follower of Jesus Christ as Lord and Savior. She was one of Jehovah's Witnesses. We shared our testimonies and witnesses with the lady, speaking of how the grace of God found only in His Son Jesus Christ became real to us when we by faith believed that Jesus was the only way of salvation. We were still praying for her to meet the real Jesus Christ as her Lord and Savior.

In the first of November, Janet and I went to do another On Mission Celebration with the folks of Trinity Baptist Church of Mooresville, North Carolina. This mission conference was the first year that the one-year-old congregation was hosting. It was a great time of sharing our God stories with these precious folks, and they truly blessed our lives hosting us with the love of our Lord Jesus Christ and in our worship experiences during the home visits with the assigned Sunday school class members and Sunday morning worship time.

At the end of November, Janet and I were in Jamestown, North Carolina, with the Life Community Church and their congregation for another Global Missions Conference. Once again, God was honored and we were blessed in every area of life and ministry. We shared the different cultures and foods from the different countries where God had called us to serve Him with our lives and gifts. We would show the children on a globe or maps where we lived around the world. We would also let them know that the children and adults were like us with a sinful nature that only Jesus Christ could forgive and change by faith and trust in Him as Lord and Savior of their lives. Many times, when we would do these mission conferences, we would take different foods, items of those countries for them to see and touch, and usually different monetary coins from these countries to give away to the children. What a joy it was to share our God stories with folks like these!

As the year 2013 was drawing to a close, Janet and I were invited to Yadkin Baptist Church in Patterson, North Carolina, to share our mission experiences with Southern Baptist folks who had given of their money and their prayers so that Janet and I could go to the nations in answer to God's call on our lives. It was a joy to thank them personally for all that they did for the over five thousand international Southern Baptist missionaries of the International Mission Board of the Southern Baptist Convention. It was a joy to tell every Evangelical Southern Baptist thanks for allowing Janet and me to go on a mission with our Lord Jesus Christ to the world to represent Him and all Southern Baptists around North America.

The following week, I went to Calvary Baptist Church in Kannapolis, North Carolina, to do a Global Mission Celebration conference with those folks. Janet, representing the Women's Missionary Union of Three Forks Baptist Church in Taylorsville, North Carolina, was doing a

Lottie Moon offering service for these folks to join over forty-three thousand other Southern Baptist folks in giving. They gave in Lottie Moon's name (she was our first missionary to China) in support of all of the International Southern Baptist Missionaries and their families as they went to live in other countries for the cause of Jesus Christ and His kingdom. The folks of Calvary Baptist Church received me with the love of Jesus Christ and thanked me for going in their name as a missionary for the Gospel of Jesus Christ. As I shared how Jesus saved me and then called me to serve Him with the precious people of Calvary Baptist Church, God honored my time with them. During commitment time, many came forward to recommit their lives to go and tell others about the grace of God only found in a personal relationship with Jesus Christ as their Lord and Savior. They were challenged to go and tell their families, their friends, their neighbors, their town of Kannapolis, the six states of Appalachia, North America, and the world as real Acts 1: 8 (NKJV) followers of Jesus Christ.

The year of 2013 proved to be an awesome year for Janet and me to be used by our Lord Jesus Christ for His glory and His Kingdom. We had been witnesses to His saving grace in many lives and to witness many say yes to His call on their lives to go and tell around the world. We were excited to see what our God and our Lord Jesus Christ would do in the year 2014!

CHAPTER 10

After the month of January in 2014, God began to send us in a mighty way to tell our testimonies of our salvation experiences and to share our God stories of telling folks on four continents about the gospel of Jesus Christ. By His leadership and guidance, we were used as evangelists and church planters to help start forty-four new Evangelical Baptist churches on four continents and give to Jesus Christ all the praise and thanksgiving for these folks.

After we returned to Taylorsville, North Carolina, to be caregivers for our oldest daughter Angela Brown and her family in 2010 while she battled kidney cancer, our Father in heaven and Jesus Christ allowed us to tell others our life story in over seventy mission conferences in North America. In addition, I went on mission with the gospel of Jesus Christ to the folks of Russia. Janet and I shared the first Sunday in February of 2014 with the folks of Clover Baptist Church of Granite Falls, North Carolina. Janet spoke first because it was the Women's Missionary Union of Clover Baptist Church who had invited us to come and to share our God stories. These folks were a blessing to us, as they encouraged us through the worship time and the fellowship time after the service and for their love gifts to our ministry. We were also told about a family who were serving with our Lord in the nations as international Southern Baptist missionaries and were members of that fellowship.

Janet and I were also able to ask the parents to join with us, as the retired international missionaries from the International Mission Board of the Southern Baptist Convention in the western area of North Carolina gathered together two or three times a year to fellowship, to pray, and to hear what our Heavenly Father was doing and had done around the world.

The next Global Missions Conference that Janet and I traveled to in February was held in Colonial Heights Baptist Church in Colonial Heights, Virginia. For six days, Janet and I shared with life groups (Sunday School classes) and the men and women of the church (I shared with a group of about twenty men, and Janet shared with the ladies of the church as part of a round table of missionaries answering questions about our ministries and as a wife of a missionary). We shared with the folks of the congregation during worship time. We witnessed many people say yes to God's call on their life to go where God would send them to serve with Him on mission with the gospel of Jesus Christ both in North America and in the nations of the world. This was an awesome time of celebration and sharing our God stories.

The next week, I traveled to Hampton, South Carolina, for a six-day Global Mission Conference with the Allendale-Hampton Southern Baptist Associations of over sixty Southern Baptist churches in this area of South Carolina. Along with the other home and international missionaries (there were fifteen units of couples and single missionaries), we shared with the Southern Baptist churches in this area, thanking them for supporting us through their giving and praying for us as well as sending each of us to serve where God had called us to serve with Him.

I was in Varnville First Baptist Church of Varnville, South Carolina, on Sunday morning to worship, preach, and share in the worship service where some committed their lives by faith to Jesus Christ as their Lord and Savior. Two people talked about their commitment to go as God's missionaries in North America and asked me to help them to know what to do in faith and obedience to God.

On Sunday night, I did the evening service with Fairfax First Baptist Church in Fairfax, South Carolina. This was an awesome time of sharing my faith and showing what God was doing in our assignment in South Africa and around the world for His kingdom. These folks were such a loving blessing to me, as was every Southern Baptist church that I shared in.

The next morning, all of our missionaries were invited to join with the seniors of these two associations to eat and to share with them at Fairfax First Baptist Church. The meal was awesome, the worship and sharing time was awesome, and the encouraging words and acts of love from these seniors touched the hearts and lives of everyone present.

On Monday night, I shared with the folks of Brunson Baptist Church of Brunson, South Carolina. The next day, I shared with the precious folk of Hampton First Baptist Church of Hampton, South Carolina, and the last day, I shared with Varnville First Baptist Church of Varnville, South Carolina.

Each day was a blessing from God to my life, and I was grateful and thankful to be used by God to thank the folks of Allendale-Hampton Association for their prayers, their love in giving so that all of us could go to serve with our Lord wherever He would send us, and those who were born again and became members of the family of God. Before we left to return to our homes, the missionaries were treated with a low-country boil consisting of seafood and fresh vegetables, which we received with thanksgiving, by the associations. This was my first time experiencing this awesome blessing from our Lord. It was all thanks to the folks of the Allendale-Hampton Baptist Association.

The last weekend of February, I was invited to do an On Mission Celebration in Gadsden, Alabama, with the Etowah Baptist Association. On the first day, all of the missionaries of each area of the world set up over thirty booths with items representing our ministries. These booths represented local evangelical and Southern Baptist ministries, North American Mission Board Southern Baptist missionaries and their ministries, and International Mission Board Southern Baptist missionaries and their ministries to the nations. The folks of over forty Southern Baptist Churches in Gadsden, Alabama, came to visit with and to talk to the missionaries about their service with the Lord and to hear what God was doing around the world.

That night during the worship service, the missionaries marched in behind the flags of the different countries of the world, and they were introduced to those present. After an awesome message from God's Word by a local pastor, many of those present were challenged to really become Acts 1:8 (NKJV) followers of our Lord Jesus Christ with many committing their lives to do so in obedience to our Lord Jesus Christ.

On Sunday, I was able to preach, to share my testimony, and to tell those present what our Lord Jesus Christ was doing and had done around the world. After doing three of these services in three Southern Baptist churches—Cross Creek Baptist Church, Immanuel Baptist Church, and Black Creek Baptist Church—at the end of the day, during the invitation and commitment time, three people believed on and trusted Jesus Christ as their Lord and Savior, and four surrendered to God's call on their lives to go as His missionaries to the world. This was an awesome time of worship, fellowship, and telling our God stories with these folks in Gadsden, Alabama.

The first of March 2014 found Janet and me sharing our testimonies and places of service while doing cross-culture ministries with First Baptist Church in Hudson, North Carolina. We thanked them for giving to the Lottie Moon Christmas offering of the Southern Baptist Convention each year so that Janet and I, along with the over six thousand single and family international Southern Baptist missionaries, could go to the nations of the world with the gospel of Jesus Christ. In addition, we shared many God stories of what our Heavenly Father was doing around the world for His name and kingdom. We were truly blessed by our brothers and sisters in Christ as we worshipped and fellowshipped together.

The last weekend of March 2014 found Janet and me in the area of Boiling Springs and Inman, South Carolina, north of Spartanburg, South Carolina, doing a Global Missions Conference with the Southern Baptist churches of the North Spartan Baptist Association of South Carolina. We were able to tell our God stories with the folks of this association north of Spartanburg, South Carolina, and to worship and do ministries with two Southern Baptist churches in Boiling Springs and Chesnee, South Carolina. During invitation time at Buck Creek Baptist Church and at Holston Creek Baptist Church in Inman, South Carolina, two people made first-time professions of faith in Jesus Christ as their Lord and Savior. Many came, recommitting their lives to Jesus Christ or to become a member of the local church.

Janet was invited back within a couple of weeks to speak at the Women's Missionary Union of the North Spartan Baptist Church annual yearly meeting at Fingerville Baptist Church in Inman, South Carolina. She is the Women's Missionary Union leader of Three Forks Baptist Church in Taylorsville, North Carolina, and has introduced many new ministries for our home church, which she talked about along with her missionary stories. It was an awesome service of her sharing her faith and ministries that she had been doing for the glory of Jesus Christ.

Next, I was asked to be at the International Mission Board table in Ridgecrest, North Carolina, for the state of North Carolina Women's Missionary Union Extravaganza held in April of 2014. I was able to share and to answer questions with many young ladies about a call of God on their lives to be a missionary serving our Lord Jesus Christ and seeking to know where He would lead them to serve. I was also able to answer many questions about going, as Janet and I were appointed as international Southern Baptist missionaries in 1996. We went to the training that was available for all Southern Baptist members seeking to obey God's call on their lives as international Southern Baptist missionaries. We would read many books and other materials about the different cultures and languages that we would learn as we lived with and ministered to people on four continents. Never did we dream that our Lord Jesus Christ would call us to each of these continents to learn not only their language but their cultures, belief systems, and various foods. God sure blessed us in every country in every area of life!

May of 2014 found Janet and me being invited to the On Missions Celebration in Sevierville, Tennessee, by by the Sevier County Baptist Association. The On Mission Conference began on Friday May 2, 2014, at the First Baptist Church of Sevierville, Tennessee, with a meet-and-greet of folks from the many Southern Baptist churches of Sevier County Baptist Association and the fifty plus local, North American Mission Board, and International Mission Board missionaries who were present and who would set up tables with their ministries for a mission fair on Saturday, May 3, 2014. There was a time of worship on both nights and a time of meeting the different folks from all the local Southern Baptist churches plus other evangelical people who were present.

All the missionaries had an opportunity to share about their ministries and give their testimonies to those who would stop at their tables to talk. This was always a personal time for those missionaries to say thanks to the people who supported their calling by God to go and serve Him wherever He led.

On Saturday morning, May 3, 2014, Janet and I shared with the folks of Walnut Grove Baptist Church of Sevierville, Tennessee, and were blessed by all who came. We always gave to the different people present a time for questions about the different cultures and the people of Brazil, South Korea, South Africa, Russia, and the other sixteen nations that we had lived and in which we had shared our faith stories for the glory of Jesus Christ and His kingdom.

On Sunday morning, May 4, 2014, we led the worship time with the folks of Jones Chapel Baptist Church of Sevierville, Tennessee. This was an awesome commitment time with many lives changed by the Holy Spirit of God. Some came to make a first-time profession of faith in Jesus Christ as their Lord and Savior. Some came to join the congregation in their service to our Lord Jesus Christ on profession of faith in Him and were led by the Spirit of God to serve Jesus Christ as a member of His church. This was another blessing of seeing and watching the Holy Spirit of God calling folks to our Heavenly Father in obedience and trusting faith in Jesus Christ. On Sunday night, Janet and I shared our God stories and thanked Red Bank Baptist Church of Sevierville, Tennessee, for their gifts to the Lottie Moon Christmas Offering and to the Cooperative Program of the Southern Baptist Convention so all International Southern Baptist missionaries could go to serve where our Lord Jesus Christ sent us. Again, the Holy Spirit of God showed up and drew all folks to Jesus Christ in obedience to His call on our lives during commitment time.

Janet and I continued to share with people while shopping in our area of North Carolina, with our children's ministries of Three Forks Baptist Church in Taylorsville, and in our Sunday school classes in Three Forks Baptist Church. Always to please our Lord, we looked to encourage many, to show the love of Jesus to widows and children, and to minister to our families in every area of Christ.

On June 19, 2014, the Russia team from Three Forks Baptist church, led by Donnie and Vicki Rogers and including Delores Fox, Kevin Taylor, Randy Gilliland, and me, began our journey to Russia, starting at Charlotte Douglas International Airport in Charlotte, North Carolina, and ending at the International Airport of St. Petersburg, Russia. We would stay at the Evangelical Seminary in St. Petersburg, Russia, while there for one day to shop for vacation Bible school materials before traveling to Novgorod, Russia, to do ministries in the area.

On Saturday June 21, 2014, we traveled to Novgorod by vans and prepared to do ministries in the different areas in and around the city. We began on Sunday morning, June 22, 2014, by doing the worship time with the Temple of the Holy Trinity in Chechulino, Russia, led by Pastor Sergei. Over the next four days, the team did vacation Bible school with the young children coming in the morning and the older children coming in the afternoon. Each time with the children, there was Bible story time, craft time, recreation time, and an assembly time, where the children would learn songs and witness a drama along with a short Bible sermon. During each Bible story time, the Word of God would be read out loud in Russian and English along with an explanation to those present of what God's Word was teaching us.

On our last day there, eighty-nine of these children professed faith in Jesus Christ as their Lord and Savior. Three of the six men who stayed and lived for six months in the rehabilitation center on the church's property studied *Experiencing God* by Dr. Henry Blackaby in Russian and committed their lives by trusting faith in forgiveness and salvation in none other than Jesus Christ as their Lord and Savior.

The team traveled to Star Russa, Russia, next to do vacation Bible schools in a local orphanage and in the Evangelical Church of the Holy Trinity in this city. At the end of the day, six of the children in these two places had prayed to receive Jesus Christ as their Lord and Savior. We were also able to visit with the local congregation to worship, fellowship, encourage the folk present, and have a wonderful meal with them.

The team next did a vacation Bible school with the Evangelical Church of the Holy Trinity in Novgorod, Russia. There were over eighty children present, and they enjoyed the crafts that they learned, which would help them in their lives. They also enjoyed their recreation time as well as hearing and learning Bible truths through Bible story time. During this time at the end of their events, using a soccer ball with the colors for visually hearing the true life of Jesus, twenty-three of those present prayed to receive Jesus Christ as their Lord and Savior for the first time. This first time with the children in this area of Novgorod, Russia, was a blessing to every member of the team, as God showed up to change hearts and lives.

The next congregation was in Valday, Russia. This was a small new congregation that had been started as a mission church of the mother church, the Evangelical Church of the Holy Trinity in Novgorod, Russia. There were over twenty children present for the vacation Bible school with three children professing faith in Jesus Christ as their Lord and Savior. This was a tourist area with many opportunities for the congregation to grow and to minister in the name of Jesus Christ in this area of Russia.

Each Sunday during the worship time in the local churches that we were ministering in, the team would share testimonies of their faith in Jesus Christ with those who were present. Brother Kevin Taylor would sing and lead the services to the glory of Jesus Christ as all present would prepare to hear the read and preached Word of God.

During the commitment time, people would commit their lives for the first time in believing in Jesus Christ as their Lord and Savior or recommit themselves to follow Him in service for Him locally, in Russia, and to the world as real Acts 1:8 (NKJV) followers of Jesus Christ!

When it was time to return to Charlotte Douglas International Airport on our flights back home, the team reflected on what we had witnessed and been a part of in service to our Lord Jesus Christ while we were on mission with God every day wherever we were. After returning to Taylorsville, North Carolina, and our families for a joyful time of rest and relaxation, the team would meet and remember all that God had done in our lives and ministries while we were gone. In a few months, as in other mission trips to Russia, we would share our God stories with pictures and personal testimonies with our local congregation at Three Forks and other Southern Baptist churches where I would do mission conferences during the year.

In August of 2014, I was invited to share my God stories with the Chipola and Alalacheeo Baptist Association Southern Baptist churches in Marianna, Florida. All missionaries who were there to serve the wonderful folks of the Baptist Association of Chipola-Alalacheeo in and around Marianna, Florida, gathered at Eastside Baptist Church, for a mission fair. Over thirty missionaries put up tables showing their places of service and spoke to the people about their ministries. It was there that I had a divine appointment to share my testimony with a mother and daughter who were contacted by the Jehovah's Witnesses and needed to ask me what they believed in in order to share their faith in Jesus Christ as their personal Lord. They also told me that our Lord Jesus Christ had sent me to help them to know what to say and do.

That afternoon, we moved our materials to First Baptist Church of Bristol, Florida, and set up tables with our ministry materials to meet and to talk to those who came. After this time, we ate a wonderful meal and then had a wonderful time with the folks from over forty Southern Baptist churches.

On Sunday morning, I preached and shared with two Southern Baptist churches in Marianna, Florida, and then on Sunday night, I preached and shared with First Baptist Church of Graceville, Florida. This Baptist church was on the campus of the Baptist College of Florida, which was in Graceville, and there were over twenty students in the worship service that night. Many talked to me about their God-called ministry to the nations of the world as His servants and how they could serve Him as Southern Baptist international missionaries. Eight of these students committed their lives to go as His missionaries during the invitation time of commitment.

During the rest of the year of 2014, I was invited to speak in worship services in Pigeon Forge, Tennessee, while on vacation in September; for Southern Baptist churches in an On Mission Celebration in Harrisburg, Illinois, in October; and in two Southern Baptist churches in Concord and Hillsborough, North Carolina. During each time of worship, folks made decisions to follow Jesus Christ as their Lord and Savior for the first time and to go on missions with and for Him wherever He would lead them. Many were encouraged with what God was doing around the world and that He was still in control of what was happening in the world.

This year of 2014 had really been one of excitement and blessings in my life and ministry. I was excited to watch what Jesus would do in my life and ministries for His glory.

From January 9 to 12, 2015, I was invited to do ministry in an On Mission Celebration in Minden, Louisiana, sharing my God stories while Janet and I served as international Southern Baptist missionaries in Brazil, South Korea, South Africa, Russia, the Czech Republic, and sixteen other countries, including those in North America.

I shared with five Southern Baptist churches of this Baptist association and was housed in the Prophet's Quarters of the First Baptist Church in Robertsville, Louisiana. Their hospitality and personal care was awesome as I stayed with them and ministered to their needs. I also did services in four other Southern Baptist churches. Many made professions of faith to Jesus Christ as their Lord and Savior, and many were encouraged to follow Jesus with their lives as His servants wherever He would lead them as real Acts 1:8 (NKJV) followers of Jesus Christ.

Janet and I were asked to share with the Catawba Valley Baptist Association at their association's annual meeting held in the First Baptist Church of Newton, North Carolina, on March 19, 2015.

We showed the DVD about our ministries in South Africa and shared our God stories concerning the various ministries that we personally witnessed God doing while we served with Him there on mission. We told about the opportunities for me to lead seven people to faith in Jesus Christ as their Lord and Savior at the large mall in Durban, South Africa. One of these folks was a young graduate of a South African university whom I met and led to personal faith in Jesus Christ. She was moving to London, England, and wanted an English Bible translation to take with her to teach English as a second language. I presented her a Bible, and we received an email from her in London, England, saying that she had joined an evangelical Bible church and had been baptized there. She thanked Janet and me for introducing her to faith in Jesus Christ and said she was now teaching English as a second language to university students. We also were honored to witness two folks from a religion that was hostile to Christians become believers and followers of Jesus Christ, who also led their families to faith in Jesus Christ.

While there on mission with our Lord Jesus Christ in South Africa, we helped to start three evangelical congregations in three different areas of Durban and Johannesburg, South Africa. We also shared about being used by Jesus to witness two unbelieving Jehovah's Witnesses become believers and followers of Jesus Christ as their personal Lord and Savior.

The personal experiences that we each had while living and serving with God in South Africa were joys and blessings in our lives and ministries.

In April, I was able to go with the men and women of Three Forks Baptist Church to help work in the North Carolina Baptist Convention Disaster Relief Building in Red Springs, North Carolina. We helped to unload and load furniture for the warehouse and for those folks in the community in need of furniture, food, and clothes. We were also able to do a steak fundraiser for a Christian man who was waiting for a liver transplant. We visited places and helped repair church buildings, homes, and other areas in need of repair. This was an awesome time of ministry and fellowship with our church family. We were used by our Lord to be a blessing to the Christian man and his family.

On June 9, 2015, I went with Donnie Rogers, Vicki Rogers, and Kevin Taylor on mission for our Lord to Novgorod, Russia, and Prague, Czech Republic, to preach in churches and do vacation Bible school with evangelical churches in both Russia and the Czech Republic.

During the worship services in Novgorod, Star Russa, Valday, and Chechulino, eight adults prayed out loud to personally receive Jesus Christ as their Lord and Savior by faith in Him, and over 140 children committed their lives to Jesus Christ by faith and received Him as their Lord and Savior during the vacation Bible school times. The team rejoiced with our Lord Jesus Christ at the personal decisions to follow Jesus Christ as His followers and believers that we were witnesses of for His glory and honor.

After many days of encouraging the folks of these four cities and loving on them with the love of Christ, we left these precious people and flew from St. Petersburg, Russia, to Prague, Czech Republic, on June 18, 2015, to be on mission with our Lord there for the first time. After arriving in Prague, Czech Republic, we were met by the pastor of the Evangelical Church of Pilsen and driven to Pilsen to stay in a local hotel and to do ministry in an Evangelical Baptist church with immigrants from Russia.

We toured the area and discussed where we could do ministries in that country in the future. On Sunday, the team led the worship time with Brother Kevin Taylor leading us to worship with music and Brother Donnie sharing a word of testimony and telling them why we were led to come on mission to do ministries in their town. Sister Vicki shared a word of testimony, and then I followed her time, leading the worship time by sharing my testimony and preaching what the Lord led me to preach. During invitation time, six adults prayed to receive Jesus Christ as their personal Lord and Savior by faith. Two of these folks were Jehovah's Witnesses who became born-again witnesses for our Lord and Savior by faith. I was also able to answer their questions and help to encourage them in their decision to become true believers and followers of Jesus Christ. We also gave them the new evangelical Bibles and helped them to learn how to read God's Word with the Holy Spirit of God directing them.

Other decisions were made in order to allow God to grow His church there and in other cities such as Prague so people could know God's saving grace through a personal relationship with Jesus Christ. Over the next four years, I went with Donnie and Vicki Rogers, Randy Gilliland, Craig Childers, and my grandson Shawn Chapman (he went in 2019) to do evangelism using vacation Bible school materials with children and adults in each church. I also preached in each church and did baby dedications (six couples with their babies), and each of us shared and taught Christian marriages and dating according to the Word of God and other Christian topics.

Shawn taught the young people of each church the Word of God and fellowshipped with them, playing games to encourage them (he was the youngest American Christian man that they had ever met who was sold out to telling others about Jesus Christ, his Lord and Savior). At the end of each trip, 130 to 150 Russian young people and adults became believers and followers of Jesus Christ. A total of over six hundred folks were added to the kingdom of God, and we helped in starting a new evangelical church.

In the almost twenty-two years Three Forks Baptist Church in Taylorsville, North Carolina, had been sending teams to Russia, we had helped start twenty-three evangelical churches in the Novgorod, Russia, area. What a joy to fellowship with and teach the folks the Word of God, to watch many commit their lives in faith to Jesus Christ as their Lord and Savior, and to follow this decision with the believer's baptism.

As an Acts 1:8 (NKJV) Baptist church, Three Forks Baptist Church goes, sends, supports in prayer and other needs, and shows them the love of Christ as part of God's family. Serving those in the Novgorod, Russia, area as brothers and sisters in Christ truly honors Jesus Christ and gives to each the joy of the Lord.

As I prayerfully conclude this work for the glory of our Lord, whom I thank for saving me, calling me to serve Him with the rest of my life until I either go to be with Him or He comes for me, I pray that this my story brings to Him glory and honor. Amen.

Jack and Janet

CONCLUSION

As I reflect on my life, I believe the only way of coming out of darkness into the light of Jesus Christ is to repent of your sins and turn to Jesus Christ by faith as your Lord and Savior. Jesus said, "I have come as a light into the world, that whoever believes in Me should not abide in darkness" (John 12:46 NKJV). I can testify to the truth of that statement! Also God's Word states in 1 John 5:11–12 (NKJV), "And this is the testimony: that God has given us eternal life, and this life is in His Son. He who has the Son has life; he who does not have the Son of God does not have life." I have His life in my heart and life! May my story lead many to saving faith in Jesus Christ.

I am the only one responsible for the contents of my autobiography and testimony in this book. No one who prints this book is responsible for the contents. I am grateful to my Lord Jesus Christ and to those who helped us in the preparation of this book.

ENDORCEMENTS

It is my joy to recommend my Brother and Sister in the Lord, Jack and Janet Burns to you, It has been my joy to serve as their pastor since becoming the pastor of Three Forks Baptist Church in 2008. Jack and Janet Burns love the Lord Jesus Christ and have spent much of their lives serving Him around the world. Jack and Janet have a great heart for missions and encourage the Body of Christ to fulfill the Great Commission found in Matthew 28: 18 – 20 (NKJV). In the pages of this book you will read of how God has used them to share the gospel of Jesus Christ and to lead others to saving faith in Christ Jesus as Lord and Savior. I pray that God will continue to use Jack and Janet to share the gospel of Jesus Christ and inspire others to do the same.

Dr. Carson Moseley
Pastor of Three Forks Baptist Church, Taylorsville, North Carolina

"But you shall receive power when the Holy Spirit has come upon you, and you shall be witnesses to me in Jerusalem, and in all Judea and Samaria, and to the end of the earth." Acts 1: 8 (NKJV). This statement has been both Jack and my vision as we said "Yes" to God's call and will for our lives. I have been blessed by my Lord Jesus Christ to serve with a man of God who has shared the gospel of Jesus Christ around the world. As you read this book, it is my prayer that all will come to know Jesus Christ as their personal Lord and Savior. (Matthew 28: 19 – 20 NKJV). Matthew 16: 24 says, "If anyone desires to come after me, let him deny himself and take up his cross, and follow me." (NKJV).

Janet Burns
Wife of Jack Burns

"Escaping the darkness of false religion by the overwhelming light of Christ's redemption," Jack Burns is a soul set free and on fire by the inescapable calling of God. Perhaps no one understands or explains better how daunting spiritual darkness attempts to eclipse the light of Christ from the view of a lost world. Like a modern day John the Baptist he has been pointing men and women to the "true Light which gives light to every man coming into the world" (John 1: 9 NKJV). For decades Jack and Janet his wife, have poured their lives into bring others to saving faith in Jesus Christ. I this autobiography you will travel through the dusty roads and stony paths of our world's most impoverished areas and also into the homes of governor's and leaders. Having seen first-hand he and Janet on the mission field, and having witnessed their life and testimony foe almost a half century, I commend them, and this treasury of memoirs, to you for a life changing experience.

Dr. Mike Runion
Pastor, City View First Baptist Church, Greenville, South Carolina.

Some of my earliest memories revolve around visits to our church by missionaries who had answered God's call to be His witnesses in foreign lands. I vividly recall the clicking and flashing of the colorful slide presentations, (for those folks younger than I am "slide presentation "may require a little bit of explanation), and the various native clothing items and artifacts displayed at the front of the sanctuary. These powerful presentations made the lives these committed men and women who lived in various locations around the world come alive to a small-town young boy. I'm glad I was raised in a mission-minded church, which strongly supported mission work around the world. And I'm thankful I learned to genuinely appreciate the personal sacrifice these missionaries exhibited by their faithfulness to serve God wherever He called them.

My admirations and appreciations for men and women who were called by God to serve as missionaries continued to grow throughout my life. I always counted it an honor and a privilege to meet and spend time with them. Little did I know that one day, God had plans to bring a Southern Baptist Convention Foreign Mission couple to be part of our local church.

As I had the privilege to meet and get to know Jack and Janet Burns, I saw in them the faithful commitment and the resolve that appeared to be consistent in all the missionaries I'd ever met. I loved to hear them share stories of what God had done for them and through them in their time spent in Brazil. Then, God called them into service again to South Korea, and later to South Africa. With each deployment came even more fascinating and remarkable accounts and testimonies.

And, whenever Jack was home, and had available time, he was always eager to join in any mission projects we were doing through our local church. When he and Janet finally retired from their Southern Baptist Convention mission work, Jack was always the first person to sign up for whatever outreach project we were planning. These have included dozens of Prison Ministry events, ministering to incarcerated men and women all across North Carolina, multiple mission trips to Kentucky, Eastern North Carolina, two mission trips to the Czech Republic, and nearly a dozen trips to Russia. I can't adequately describe how significant it has been to have a "Genuine Foreign Missionary" as part of our team on all these excursions.

If there is one trait that stands out in Jack's life, I would undoubtedly say that it is his faithfulness in sharing the gospel of Jesus Christ. No one has ever spent more than a couple of minutes around Jack without hearing how God changed him from a false witness into a born-again Soul Winner. Wherever Jack goes, folks are always amazed at how God has used him and used Janet in such a mighty way. People all over the world are fascinated as Jack recalls some of what he and Janet have been able to witness. Almost invariably, as Jack shares his testimony and accounts of God's greatness, someone will tell him, "You really need to write a book about what God has done in your life."

Well....I think he finally got the message! I believe in addition to the many request from other folks, God finally stepped in and let Jack know it was time to transcribe some of what He had allowed Jack and Janet to witness.

I know you will find this book as fascinating and inspiring as the other folks I've seen touched by Jack's testimony around the world. May reading this book inspire all of us to commit our lives fully to His will and His way, and to embolden us to share the Gospel with everyone we have a chance to meet.

Donnie Rogers
member of Three Forks Baptist Church

Printed in the United States
by Baker & Taylor Publisher Services